WORK AND PLAY

Owing to the antiquity and rarity of this book, certain pages are regrettably absent, and readability is compromised due to the blurring of the original text. If you possess any insights regarding the availability of these missing sections, kindly inform us. Your assistance is crucial in ensuring the completion of this significant work for the benefit of future generations.

WORK AND PLAY

IN INDIA AND KASHMIR

J D GORDON

GYAN

Published by

Gyan Publishing House
5, Ansari Road
Daryaganj, New Delhi-110002
Phone: 011-47034999, 9811692060
E-mail: books@gyanbooks.com

Distribution Network
gyanbooks.com
India, USA, Canada, UK, Australia

ISBN: 978-93-7097-880-5 (PB)
First Published, 1893

2nd Impression 2025

Printed at: Gyan Press, Delhi.

WORK AND PLAY
Author J D Gordon

WORK AND PLAY IN INDIA AND KASHMIR

WORK AND PLAY

IN INDIA AND KASHMIR

BY

J D GORDON

Barrister-at-Law

EDEN, REMINGTON & CO

LONDON AND SYDNEY

1893

Dedicated

TO

MY MOST LOVING AMANUENSIS,

"BABY."

INTRODUCTION.

HUMILIATING though it may be, I am bound to confess that the following pages have neither hero, heroine or moral!

A barrister, about to try his luck in India, may possibly, by hard study of them, evolve some useful information, but if the more frivolous reader can herewith beguile a leisure hour my object has not been in vain.

CHAPTER I.

Every profession has and talks its own "shop," which, though doubtless of great interest to the members thereof, is, as a rule, unbearable to the outside world.

Now I have been told that of all kinds the most unendurable is law "shop," and have consequently in the following pages endeavoured, as far as possible, to eliminate it.

My object is to give a slight sketch of the life a young barrister will lead who seeks his fortune up-country, as the Indian expression is; and as all work and no play makes Jack a dull boy, a few sketches of his social life and amusements must not be considered misplaced.

With these few words of explanation let us at once plunge *in medias res.*

The work of a barrister residing in Calcutta, Bombay, or Madras differs but little from that of his stay-at-home brethren, but it is when he wanders further inland and away from the great centres of Indian civilization that a marked change is noticeable.

Solicitors disappear, and he is face to face with his client. This, of course, necessitates a thorough knowledge of the language, no light task, as many have found to their cost.

Instead of a neat little bundle of papers all "copied in a big round hand" he will probably be handed a few dirty documents in the vernacular, from which, with perchance a few facts elicited from the client, he may now proceed to construct a brief.

Oh, glib-tongued gentlemen who would merge the two professions into one, would that on a blazing day in June I could sit you down to prepare a brief out of such materials. *Ne sutor ultra crepidam* would soon be the burden of your cry!

To go into Court imperfectly instructed is, to a barrister with proper pride in his profession, a foretaste of purgatory. Questions from the bench, requiring immediate answer; misstatements of the opposite side, needing prompt correction; reference to documents somewhere—but where?—on the record, all combine to make him pine for a well-prepared brief and a solicitor to prompt reply and hand the right paper, thus leaving counsel free to attend entirely to the vital points of the case undisturbed.

Whether due to imperfect instructions or to a physical incapacity for accuracy the native legal practitioner must be very closely watched from start to finish, his statement of facts being at times positively alarming, and his power of misreading documents prodigious. I am not, let me say at once, unaware that a few brilliant exceptions exist, but speaking generally the native legal practitioner is unreliable as a junior, and treacherous as an opponent.

Under the heading "legal practitioner" must be brought first Barristers; these are English-speaking native gentlemen who have studied in England, and been called to the Indian bar. Till quite lately their ranks were recruited entirely from among the well-born; but alas, more than one "chamār" name now graces the law list.

In the second place we come to the "High Court Vakil, or Pleader." The examination these gentlemen have to pass is very severe, and though the youngest barrister may claim to lead the most venerable vakil, he will often show good sense and courtesy in allowing his experienced junior to conduct the case, whilst remaining carefully at hand to assume any responsibility which may arise, that being a very weak point in native armour.

Next in rank we find "Vakils of the District Judge's Court," either young men who must work in this position for some years before presenting themselves for High Court examination, or elder men whose ambition soared no higher than making a competence close to their home. Many of them are of the greatest assistance when acting more or less as solicitors, whereas others are of the worst type of nonsense talkers, the bane and curse of many an overworked district officer. Below these we come upon the "Mukhtyārs" or "agents," of whom, as a rule, the less said the better.

Spreading a small carpet under some friendly tree, they lie in wait for guileless villagers on their way to Court, and once in such a spider's web, "farewell, a long farewell" to all ideas of truth and right; forgery and perjury will be supplied upon the lowest possible terms.

It is mainly from this class that the "dalāls" come.

A word as to these dalāls or brokers; they are the honest barrister's bugbear, and many are the attempts made to suppress them; their *modus operandi* is pretty much the same in all cases; two or three men are shown into your office, their case seems good, they are willing to pay a proper fee, they retire to get the money or to consult; one of them reappears, and with much circumlocution informs you that the disposal of the case is in his hands, and what may he expect from your honour? When informed that "the sahib gives no dusturi," *i.e.*, percentage on the amount of the fee, he smiles an evil smile, and marches the would-be clients off to some less scrupulous market.

The payment of any gratuity to these dalāls is a penal offence, but "tell it not in Gath," thousands batten and fatten upon this mode of obtaining a livelihood.

The truth is, it was a silly mistake to legislate on the subject. If professional pride and self-respect are not strong enough to keep men from purchasing work in a shameless way, it would have been better to let them cut each others throats in a competition as to who would pay the most dustūri, which in a very short time would have produced such a state of things as to bring in its train a radical cure.

Of course the dalāl rarely boldly asks for dustūri, thereby keeping outside the letter of the law; hint and innuendo, given with true oriental cleverness, are all you have to work on, and should you try running him in on these you will gain some experience in holding an eel by its tail, and make deadly enemies galore.

Now, when you consider that the commonest transactions of life amongst natives are, as a rule, carried out by brokers, it is evident that even to the best and most honourable amongst them this prohibition of "dalāli" seems wrong and uncalled for. Each banker pays dalāli, each tradesman, each servant seeking service, each giver of a nautch or other "tamāsha" employs and pays it; your own head servant, be he

Hindu or Mahomedan, is considered as the middleman to your favour and gets his "dustūri" on every rupee you spend; why then (so argues the native mind) should we not employ a broker to help us in the real hard work of litigation? Why, indeed, and why should not a fixed fee be paid them openly, without concealment?

As things are at present, these men exercise well-nigh unlimited power, and many a young barrister has to see case after case lost to him through their evil practices; of course, successful seniors do not suffer so much, as their work is to a great extent sent by vakils of good position, or brought to them direct by old clients.

To understand how completely "dalāli" is part and parcel of Indian life one needs some knowledge of and insight into the native character, and may I say it with all humility, nay, trembling, that it is a thing rarely, very rarely obtained nowadays by Anglo-Indians.

I can imagine the scorn with which this idea will be treated by many who have perhaps been years in India, but bear with me a moment, and let me ask, When do you see the native as he is? When do you, laying aside rank and office, be they what they may, speak with him as to an equal, all fear laid aside, all patronage or favours desired, completely out of sight?

My dear sir, if you are a civilian, your Indian education from the first day of your service was in the hands of the police, or of their devoted slaves, the various petty court officials, on whom you, a boy, practically ignorant of the language, despite your intimacy with Forbes' grammar and the Bagh-o-bahar, must rely *in toto*; and who led you along a beaten path, certainly not leading to a true insight into native character. Why, the Tommy Atkins of sporting proclivities, speaking an extraordinary lingo to the villagers he meets, knows more than you do, and will perchance make himself better understood than you, with your high-flown, grammatical sentences. Army men make little or no pretence of getting to know the "niggers," as they generally term the natives, unless they turn to the staff, but forest officers, indigo planters, and others come directly in contact with their subordinates. On the whole, however, I doubt if any Europeans can get on such intimate terms with all classes, educated and uneducated, as the barrister who has really mastered the language, and is able to turn his "munshi" out of the room and converse with his clients on every subject that may crop up. A political argument may arise. Mahomedans love a religious discussion; Brahmins are delighted to instruct you on the "vedas;" old soldiers spin yarns of the mutiny; endless are the topics which will form a pleasant digression after work, and in such free and easy converse the real character is laid bare to an observant eye. "Alas, sahib," said a rich zamindar to me, "why cannot I talk to the collector sahib as I do to you, but in his presence my heart turns to water." The said collector was a hop-o'-me-thumb, the son of a head waiter in a well-known west end restaurant, and as a natural consequence a very important person.

To support my contention I venture to introduce some sketches of natives I was well acquainted with, and doubt if in any employment under Government it would have been possible for me to have had such a pot-pourri of native friends.

MANIKCHAND, GENERAL DEALER.

To see the old man squatting humbly in a small shop in the Sudder bazaar, bargaining keenly over a few annas, you would scarcely believe that any bank between Peshawur and Bombay, *viâ* Allahabad, would honour his cheque for six or seven lacs, or that a visit to the rooms above his shop would be repaid by the sight of the most exquisite Kashmir shawls, Delhi jewellery, Agra embroidery, not to mention Chinese and Japanese curios. But so it is, and I have spent many an hour in that room, which has a small window overlooking the busy street.

My friendship for old Mānikchand came about through the death of his only son, a bright, handsome young fellow who used to come and consult me about reading for the bar. On his death-bed he asked his father to send me a handsome Satzuma plate as a souvenir—the poor old man soon after came to see me and brought it.

The loss of an only son is in all lands a bitter grief, but to a Hindu father the loss of an only son is a matter for terror. Who will set fire to his funeral pyre? Who will present the sacred cake? And who at the stated feasts perform the ceremonies whereby after due purification the Hindu soul obtains rest?

The old man talked long and bitterly, but

cheered up after a while, and I found him a most clever, pleasant companion, subsequent experience only strengthening that impression.

We had some tremendous arguments about the right treatment of this son's widow, a pretty little maiden fourteen years old. According to the vile custom she was deprived of her jewels and bade to weep and mourn till a merciful death should release her; but I am glad to say that, after much argument, the old bigot consented to admit a lady from the Zenāna Mission, who found means to brighten up the child widow's lot in some degree.

Mānikchand had the most blood-curdling notions as to the morality of the average British matron, and his account-books certainly are some excuse for his error.

"Credit Mrs. Sheepseyes Rs. 1,000, deb. acc. of Mr. Topsawyer, C.S.;" "20yds. Azimgarh satin for Mrs. X., deb. acc. Captain Shooster;" and so on for pages on end; kya mūtlub, sahib?

In vain I tried to persuade the old heathen of the holiness and beauty of platonic affection. He replied in proverbs which scarce bear translating.

For the competition wallahs of the present day, as compared to the civilians of his youth, his dislike is unlimited. "Wah! wah! where are the houses and carriages of thirty years ago?"

For the British officer, here to-day and gone to-morrow, he has a holy awe, manifesting itself in a preference for his cash to his credit. But the real bugbear of my old friend is the Bengāli Bābu. I happened to be in the room one day, when two young Bābus, in European dress, oiled and curled to the —nth, entered. They spoke vile Urdu, and Mānikchand pretended not to understand a word they said, taking care to speak himself in the swiftest and most involved manner. The Bābus tried English, and—alas! for veracity—the old scamp swore he "Angrezi nehīn janta" (knew not English).

The greasy Bengālis departed, and Mānikchand relieved his feelings by going to the door and expectorating. He subsequently in a low sing-song consigned all Bengālis, their cousins, uncles, and aunts to a place known on the map as Jehannum.

I have been repeatedly scolded for my improvident and extravagant habits, but by no one so persistently as by this wily Hindu. He has even pointed out to me that the fault lay with my careless bringing up. "If you sahibs were taught in childhood the value of money you would not throw it away so recklessly; if, as with us, the babe just able to crawl were given a box to rattle, containing pice; if daily he were made to perform puja to the money rattle; if, as he grows older, he were allowed to change the collected pice into silver coins, then would his soul be filled with respect and awe for money." This is the wisdom of Mānikchand. How can I, a pauper, gainsay him? Wise or not, many a tradesman might take a leaf out of Mānikchand's book in dealing honourably and fairly. His wares are good, his promise reliable, and his manners perfection.

THE NAWĀB.

The title of Nawāb conjures up visions of embroidered garments of purple and fine linen; but, alas! my Nawāb had none of these things. He was poor—bitterly poor—and, as is so often the case, proud and touchy beyond words.

Tall, well-made, with keen, fearless eyes, he would have graced any position as an "anax andrôn," but his retainers were dwindled to three ragged-looking rascals sorely in need of shekels.

Our acquaintance began out pig sticking, when I was much struck by the fearless riding and dexterity of the Nawāb; instead of using a spear he used a tulwar with deadly effect.

Our friendship was further cemented by my successfully defeating his bitterest foe, a

Hindu Mahājan, who held a decree against some of the few acres remaining to him; the decree-holder's pleader made an ass of himself, and, before the error could be put right, the dirty old decree became time-barred. Great tears stood in the young man's eyes as he thanked me, and, warned by bitter experience, he tried hard to keep out of the money-lender's clutches.

After this the Nawāb constantly dropped into my office for a chat, and even helped me to interview clients, who in a truly marvellous way would confide to him secrets which neither I nor my Munshi could have got at. He would have succeeded brilliantly at the bar, but the mere idea of having to sit beside a Bengāli Bābu was too much for his feelings, and he preferred his poverty and independence.

I went to dinner with the Nawāb once, *tête-à-tête*; his wife cooked some of the sweets with her own hands, and I was permitted to thank her through a thick purdah.

We wretched Europeans simply don't know what a properly cooked pillao is, and as for curry, " Ye gods and little fishes ! "

The cloth was spread on the floor, and we faced each other sitting cross-legs; around us were placed numberless small, covered dishes, from which I was pressed to choose, and choose again. One of the sweets was an apple preserved whole, and wrapped in silver tissue; it was undeniable. After dinner we smoked and argued, the Nawāb maintaining gravely that the Government of India would be better managed if, instead of employing the cheap and dirty Bābu, the respectable but impecunious Mussulman were given a chance. To this I replied, " The objectionable Bābu learns English; your co-religionists do not," but my adversary smote me hip and thigh by suggesting that if the work of all Government Offices and High Courts were in the local vernacular it might be more conducive to justice. I felt that to cope with such a radical was beyond my powers.

If ever, urged on by some heaven-forsaken Gladstone-trained Government, we leave India to govern itself, may I be there to see men like the Nawāb raise the stern war cry of Islam, and with one mighty effort sweep the cringing Bengali off the face of the land; and woe in that day to the money-lender and extortioner.

NIYASHI TAWAIF.

Had I any character to lose, the mere fact of admitting so much as a nodding acquaintance with this fair one would blast my chances of keeping it; what, then, if I plead guilty to knowing her well? When her jewels, valued at Rs. 45,000, were stolen and found in the house of an ex-lover, she desired me to prosecute him, and was with great difficulty made to understand that I never appeared for a prosecution; but when the scamp contrived by some hocus-pocus in a native magistrate's court to get acquitted and ran her in for bringing a false charge against him it was time to interfere.

To the terrible disgust of my lordly Munshi, Miss Niyashi would drive up to the bungalow and send in Salaam; being a girl from Delhi she spoke the most delicious Urdu, clear and sonorous, and being, further, a young lady of considerable powers of observation, her remarks were worth hearing. After much litigation we brought the ex-lover down heavily, to the tune of three years' imprisonment and a large fine as well.

Great was the joy of Niyashi; nothing but the Munshi's lowering eye prevented her giving me a grateful kiss, though, as she had just been chewing cardamums, I did not lose much.

If a native woman is not nibbling cardamums, she is on to the betel, or failing these sucking hard at a hubble bubble, so that it is easy to conceive what their breath must amount to! Revenons to our lost lamb.

It was a matter of faith with the young native mashers that she sang divinely; as a matter of fact, the sounds she produced resembled a steam whistle practising Wagner, or a naughty girl getting toko from her awful dad; but what on earth does that matter so long as golden bangles and nose-rings are the reward? "Prosit," my dusky Patti; tip us another squall. When, however, your throat is dry, rest awhile, and chaff your admirers, an art you are well-nigh perfect in.

Niyashi sings and dances no more now! She is a Purdanashin lady! Not only in Germany is vice allowed to become a virtue, in India too the successful dancing girl finds a husband and rest for her old age. Sweet, shrieking sisterhood, here is a chance for you; give poor Tommy Atkins a rest; you have done him all the harm possible. Come and scratch my eyes out for daring to speak of a nautch girl as a friend.

Faugh! you sexless, bloodless harpies;

may you get a due reward in a future state, and may it be all I desire!

BEGUM SAHIBA.

First she telegraphed, then she wrote a long incoherent letter, and finally she sent her "Mukhtyār," from all of which I gathered that my fair client the Begum had been getting into some fresh scrape. She was a perfect genius at doing so.

Either she was refusing to dismiss her far too numerous retainers when so ordered by the Collector Sahib, or she was resisting the execution of a decree of Court, bidding her demolish a wall she had built on a neighbour's land; or, worse still, inciting her servants to soundly wollop a too importunate creditor!

But the Begum and I were sworn allies, and as fast as a night in the train and relays of horses could bring me I was at her house, ready for a long talk through the purdah (a most annoying arrangement). The matter was serious; a man had been murdered close to her gates, and, as ill luck would have it, he was the servant of a neighbouring Rajah, with whom for years past the Begum had been at daggers drawn.

It was a real pleasure to talk to this lady, firstly because she spoke such exquisite Urdu, and secondly because she was one of the clearest headed persons it has been my luck to encounter.

To spare my reader shop, I need only say that the luckless corpse involved the Begum in three cases, two criminal and one civil.

Scandal was often busy with the dear Begum's name; "she had murdered her husband; she had lovers by dozens; she forged and used documents;" and so on by the yard, but Dogberry shall answer.

"Marry, sir, they have committed false reports, and moreover they have spoken untruths; secondarily, they are slanders; sixth and lastly, they have belied a lady; thirdly, they have verified unjust things; and to conclude, they are lying knaves."

But would you know why we are such friends? The Begum has a wee little girl, just five years old, and still too young to observe the purdah. Now this maiden is to marry me (she herself is my authority); and truly if the fairy in silk sari, who sits on my knee and begs for one more story, grows up as beautiful as she now is, I might do worse. Good-bye, little nut brown maid, may your life behind the accursed purdah be as bright and guileless as that of the gaily plumaged bird captive in yonder gilded cage.

GAURI LAL, SHUNKER LAL, MAHĀJUNS.

If you come through the main gate and keep straight on to the corner where the Lohari gully cuts across the Chandni Chowk, you may notice a stout man seated in the small shop to your right.

A clean white cloth is stretched over the floor, and the only merchandise apparent consists of half-a-dozen large account books bound in coarse red cloth.

No banker's clerk need be ashamed of the beautifully written sheets over which Gauri Lal is poring; each line of the square symmetrical Hindi characters has been written up with the cleanest cut reed pen by men whose whole life has been devoted to such work.

There is nothing in the poor and plain surroundings of the little shop to suggest any ideas of wealth; nevertheless, this is a branch firm of the bank whose ramifications spread from Meerut to Benares. Watch this fat Dalāl broker, who has just rolled out of his tikka gharri (I beg his pardon, it is not tikka, the shandradan is his private property), how carefully he removes his shoes before venturing to cross the threshold, how deeply he salaams, how rapidly he whispers the magic formula of the bank rates current that day, and how eagerly he hurries away when his orders have been given him!

He is off now to worry the agent of the Bank of Bengal, who will either damn his eyes or welcome him effusively as he does or does not want to do business.

From early dawn till mid-day Gauri Lal will sit solemn as the Hindu god he so much resembles, then for two hours disappear for his well-earned sleep; whether he then works till sunset or far on into the night depends upon business.

If work has to be done he will be there to do it.

But what of Shunker Lal? Own brother though he be to Gauri Lal, yet must we seek for him elsewhere.

Whilst his stout brother sits weaving his net in the bazaar, the slim and graceful Shunker Lal, arrayed in finest linen and bedecked with rings of price, is passing rapidly from town to town in the N.W.P., negotiating here a loan, there a mortgage, here dunning a tardy debtor, there executing a Court decree.

No idler he, and in spite of his low, soft voice and silky manner, not a man to be trifled with.

To-morrow will be a big Hindu festival, and the brothers, who are my good friends and pleasantest of clients, have invited me out to their celebrated garden residence.

Three miles out of cantonments, on the Sikundra road, you will see a vast wall-enclosed garden, in the heart of which stands a large stone-built house, from the flat roof of which the eye may travel over the Mosques and minarets of the town to the great red fort, and away beyond to the shining Jumna and its priceless pearl, the Taj.

Here, in deep and secluded calm, is the home of the Mahājuns. Here their white-headed old father divides his time pretty equally between playing with his grand-children and making his soul; a most courteous old gentleman, as you will find, but with somewhat hazy notions as to railways and telegraphs.

"Būndaghi, Ram Ram, Sahib," pipe in welcome two little boys, gaily robed and decked with many bangles.

Profiting by former experience, they promptly attack my coat pockets and produce, amid squeals of delight, sundry painted Christmas and birthday cards, with which booty they rush off madly to the Zenana to display their treasures.

After this stormy welcome, we are taken up to the flat roof and comfortably installed in long deck chairs, of undeniable Bombay pattern; fresh picked oranges and plantains from the garden below, together with a tray of home-made sweets (rather different these to the sticky-looking messes sold in bazaars) are spread for our delectation.

We discussed the Russian advance, the falling rupee, the plenteous harvest, the last vagary of our Municipal Council, the chances of a riot in the Mohūrrum, and endless other topics, till the sun died away and the swift-travelling Indian night overtook us.

The friendship these native gentlemen professed for me stood the test of a pretty severe strain, when young Spavin, of the 4th Slashers, made such a terrible fool of himself over poker, contriving to drop a cool Rs. 4,000 in one night.

The lad came to me with a long face, as the money had to be paid before the end of the week, and his available assets would scarcely have realized half that amount.

"The governor will see me through all right," he said, "but that means a six weeks' delay."

Not having at the time any money available, I went down to Gauri Lal and explained matters to him; without any hesitation, he advanced me Rs. 4,000, on my note of hand, and on my repaying the amount with the paternal Spavin's remittance he refused to receive any interest at all, politely assuring me that friendship was more than a hundred per cent.

Try this test of friendship on some of your banker acquaintances, and kindly let me know if it is successful.

THE HORSE DEALER.

Some people said that the term horse-stealer would better describe my friend Afzul Khan, but this was a gross libel and only manifested their extreme ignorance.

Oh, dear, no; whatever might be said as to his professional conduct, the source thereof was pure.

Afzul Khan and I are sworn "bhais" (brothers), and he always lets me know of the arrival of a new batch of ponies so as to give me the first pick.

As soon as I have decided on an animal, it is at once sent up to my house, and the price is only discussed some days later, thereby keeping up the fiction that everything that belongs to Afzul Khan belongs to me, but this friendship was not of immediate growth, and it was only after I had caught my worthy friend in two distinct attempts to stick me that he became my brother true.

The first of these was with a smart-looking Waziri mare, and he nearly landed me. Sound, smart, and cheap—what more could I want? I took a pin and gently pricked the coronet of the off fore; no response. Again harder; dead as a door-nail; the mare was unnerved. Without a word he jumped on her back, and fled from the wrath to come. The second attempt was with a long, likely-looking animal, measuring an easy 13.2 (the then polo height); well-bred, and a picture, but somehow "I hae'd ma doots."

"Be on the racecourse at five a.m. sharp to-morrow, and we can try a spin together," said I, and there he was in due time.

He rode the tat for sale, and I a steady little Arab; the tat could travel, and Afzul Khan left me far behind.

He exulted wildly, and made sure that the handsome flyer was sold. I dismounted and bade him do likewise; my Syces led the horses up and down in view; Afzul Khan looked anxious, but accepted a cigarette and we discussed terms; the animals got cooler and cooler, and when quite cool were trotted past. Alas for the dealer; the "coolth" after the heat betrayed a decided dot and go one; again my now "bhai" rode away disgusted.

Scamp he doubtless was, but, oh, how he could ride! and how well he looked! He rode the wildest looking devils in a plain snaffle, and in a short time he could say, with apparent truth, "Gharīb, bilkul gharīb," and if the purchaser did not find the animal quite so quiet, why, as John Jorrocks says, "Lord love you, sir; I can sell you an 'orse, but I can't sell you 'ands."

Afzul Khan has two brothers, one of whom collects the animals over the border and rails them down to Lahore, four hundred at a time, in cattle vans. There the second brother receives, and proceeds to smarten up and educate the new arrivals. This done they are drafted down country to wherever the demand for ponies is greatest.

A smart cavalry regiment generally gets the pick of the basket, and "many a gallant plunger can say that Afzul Khan is a most patient creditor, if treated politely, and not as a d—d nigger."

Farewell, my unprincipled Bhai, never again shall I, at early dawn, gallop your screws round the dewy racecourse, or school them over the mud walls beyond; never again will you sit in the moonlight and tell me tales of life as seen by you in many wanderings, but in this dull and lonely life memories of our friendship come at times to cheer.

ABDUL GAFFAR, MUNSHI.

As a rule the sons of Mahomedans who were once well-to-do find nothing better to occupy their time than to worry the powers that be with endless petitions for employment under Government, utterly regardless of the fact that their ignorance unfits them for any position of trust. My friend Abdul Gaffar had begun this profitless occupation, but his lucky star brought him into contact with a certain Collector, whose family name must *per se* identify him with the highest traditions of our Indian history; a few sensible words showed the luckless aspirant that his time would be better spent learning English fluently, and law in its many branches.

I was in want of a clerk, and at the Collector's recommendation tried his *protégé;* in a very short time the desired fluency in English began to manifest itself unpleasantly, as when he gravely told a magistrate that a certain thing was "beer and skittles!" and further his language became "painful and frequent and free." *Mea culpa! mea,* or else why did "the courteous George" one day say reprovingly, "My dear fellow, your language savours more of the camp than of the forum!" Neat?

Munshi Sahib, as we called him, was a great success, and we became great friends; he threw himself heart and soul into improving my knowledge of Urdu, in furtherance whereof he introduced me to his father, a most charming old gentleman, who had lost his all in the mutiny owing to his unswerving loyalty. His timber yards in Cawnpore and Meerut were set on fire, and he himself had a narrow shave.

Doubtless with intent to further improve my vernacular, Abdul Gaffar carried me off night after night to nautches given by native gentlemen, but the English-speaking guests were so numerous that this form of study had to be abandoned; besides, the smell of attar of roses so terribly prevalent on these occasions kills me dead.

For three years the Munshi stayed with me, in which time we had thoroughly learned to know and trust each other, but then came advancement for him. His friend the Collector had become a Commissioner; he remembered Joseph, and made him his head clerk or "sheristadār." Four years of hard honest work saw my good friend a full-fledged Deputy-Collector, and the gods alone know what further greatness awaits him. *Macte virtute, Munshiji!* May you in your prosperity remain the courteous gentleman it was my pleasant fortune to know.

GULAB, SYCE.

Everyone in the station knew the "Long 'un," and as Gulab was the factotum of that worthy—we all knew Gulab. When Mahomedans condescend to be syces they make good ones, but of all natives, Hindu or Mahomedan, this man was the best syce upon record. His father had held some land in the Azimgarh district, but the money lenders had filched it away bit by bit, and the son wisely preferred service to starvation. As head syce to the "Long 'un" he got good wages and ruled the grass-cutters and syces with considerable severity.

Although willing to admit that his master knew something about horses—as well he might—Gulab entertained a scarce-concealed belief that all remaining knowledge on this subject was embodied in his person, and grand were the rows he used to have with the numerous Cabul dealers who brought round animals for his master's inspection.

To know more about the noble animal than a Cabuli—whether as to riding it or doctoring it—is to know a good deal. Once up at Simla a grey-bearded dealer rode down the steep winding pathway leading to the Rockcliff Hotel, and would sell us his smart-looking pony. Gulab, as the captious critic, suggested "spavin"—the old man's eyes flashed evilly, and without a word he turned and cantered up the zigzag path, till, reaching the top, he wheeled round and galloped furiously down, reining up sharp within a few feet of us. "Does that look like spavin, you monkey-face with the brains of an owl?" was his indignant answer.

Strange it is, but most men fancy themselves greatly on what is far from being their strong point, and so Gulab, who can give most men any points in cleaning, clipping, and turning out properly any horse in his charge, must play at vetting and get snubbed.

No notice of this good fellow would be adequate which failed to praise his own home-made "momrōgen" for cleaning brown leather! Wild horses could not drag the secret from him. His Sahib's harness and riding boots were the jealous wonder of the place; this was right and proper, but a day came when the right to use this precious polish was conferred on me, unworthy though I am, for a relative of Gulab managed to get himself into a serious scrape in Azimgarh, out of which it was my luck to pull him. From and after this time the Long 'un boots had a rival!

To further cement our friendship Gulab, by a wonderful bit of smartness, saved—if not my life—at least several bones by dragging me from under an overturned dogcart.

With so many connecting links the chain of friendship was soon forged, and though he is not one of earth's great ones, his goodwill and affection are, I trow, as valuable as if his puggari were studded with jewels and his titles swept the ground in his train.

BHUP SINGH, THAKUR.

The Thakur class do not, as a rule, go out as servants, but dear old Bhup Singh was my "durwan" (door-keeper), and one of his sons my favourite "chuprassi" (messenger). Both father and son were over six foot high, and curled up their long moustaches in an alarming fashion; but of far more value to me than their personal appearance was the true-hearted nature of their service—night and day one or the other was within call. Luckily for me the old man chose to sleep outside my door, as he was able to seize a madman who had crept into the house, and was in the act of swinging an iron-bound latti over my head as I slept.

Bhup Singh's story was a sad one. Twenty-five years before he came into my service he was a well-to-do Zamindar, proud of his pretty wife and two bonny boys. Whilst working one day he heard screams from a field near by. To seize his heavy latti and rush to the spot was the work of a minute; but, alas, it had not needed long for a savage old boar to knock down and rip open the luckless little wife. Frenzied at the sight, Bhup Singh attacked the brute and battered it to death.

The Brahmins, when consulted, told the wretched husband that as his wife had been in death defiled by contact with an unclean animal it would go hard with her—prayers well paid for being her only chance. Bhup Singh spent Rs. 4,000 in prayer, and the money lender had him and his land in deadly grip.

It was as a client that I made the old man's acquaintance, and when he at length realized that there was no way out of his troubles he went away in silence. A few days later he returned with his son and spoke thus: "Through the mercy of your laws my two sons and I have now one shred of land left, which yields us five rupees a month. Upon that my eldest son can work and live, but as for my worthless self and this son of mine may we not be your servants?"

I was very proud of my handsome old Durwan, and, despite his village patois (gomari), had much talk with him.

During five years all went well, but fate had more grief in store for Bhup Singh. Cholera was raging. In the morning one of my syces died, and by mid-day I was sent for again. This time it was my old friend's son who lay in agony. We tried hard to save him, but a native will not fight for life. He lets himself die, and soon the poor fellow was at rest. Bhup Singh returned home to wait patiently till the grim spirit should seize him by the hair, and speed him to whatever mystery awaits the faithful Hindu.

> "Dear master, I can go no further,
> Here lie I down and measure out my grave."

CHAPTER II.

A GLANCE back at the last chapter makes me terribly afraid someone will exclaim, "But Philip chatter'd more than brook or bird." But pardon me this once, and the remainder of the tale shall feel the spur.

To work as a barrister you must settle down somewhere. Now, where is it to be? Have you a little money? Then try Allahabad—seat of the N.W.P. High Court. Lots to be made in time. Yes, in time! As a sarcastic judge remarked of this place, "There are more dogs than bones, and some bones are scarcely fresh!" Most insulting, but, alas! the warning should not be despised.

The successful seniors do well, but the junior bar are terribly pressed by "heathen cheap labour."

Lucknow, the Chief Court of Oude, attracts many, and splendid fees are still paid by the wealthy Talookdars, while the social joys of this station far exceed those of any up-country rival. The climate is, beyond doubt, better than that of Allahabad; escape to the hills in case of illness far easier.

Of Lahore, in the Punjaub, I can only speak from hearsay. There is a strong Bar there, many of its members doing splendidly, but how it fares with the struggling junior I know not.

These three towns invite the man who can wait; he who cannot must try Meerut, Bareilly, Agra, Delhi, or some such place, where, rivals being fewer, work of some kind soon falls to his share.

"Less money, more fun," should be the motto of such stragglers. Polo and racquets, an occasional day's pig-sticking or shooting must serve as a set-off to the heavier fees made in headquarters.

A good-natured magistrate will, when possible, adjourn cases so as to suit all parties, he having lots of other work ever ready.

In moderation, then, the local barrister may amuse himself far more than his High Court friends, who are forced by competition to pay more respect to popular opinion, as represented by the Vakil element, through whom work filters to the bar. A Vakil is utterly unable to understand or appreciate our British capacity for combining brain and muscle, work and play; solemnity is with him a synonym for wisdom. If once dubbed by the native a "kehlne-wallah," or a man who likes to play, you must rub hard and long to efface the stain cast on your professional escutcheon. "But yet the pity of it, Iago."

In no country is good hard exercise so much needed as in India. Is it likely that a cranky man with swollen liver can do such work as a sound in wind and limb product? Besides, do look at facts. Who is the best barrister in Bombay? Ask the man in the street. What income is that barrister making? £25,000 a year! How many tiger did he kill? More than all the Vakils would care to eat, even *cum grano.*

Tiger-shooting takes more time than a stray bit of pig-sticking, and polo never begins before 4.30 p.m., so, briefless, rush home, slip into breeches and boots, rattle off to the polo ground, but, for heaven's sake, learn the rules, and don't cause a good fellow's death by crossing or standing over the ball!

Bombay sets a good example, yet is the Mufassal not utterly benighted. Begin at the beginning. Where can you find a better shot than our Chief Justice in Allahabad? Who has long been the champion racquet-player of the N.W.P., if not of India? Who but the "courteous George," whose winning address has pulled so many an appeal out of the fire?

Finally, does not Allahabad rejoice in one so learned in the law that his brethren all bow down to him; yea, they beg a morsel of advice from him not unfrequently! But, *ea fama vagatur*, that on a certain blazing day in April he rode out upon a long-tailed Arab horse, and did, in company with an illiterate subaltern of sporting appearance, give battle to no fewer than eight wild boar, vulgarly known as pig, of which they did slay five. An unholy proceeding, indeed, and one of which, let us hope, he is now much ashamed!

How about that smart four-in-hand in Lucknow? Is the driver of it less capable of conducting a case than his solemn and portly rival who takes his "hawa khana" or mouthful of fresh air in a landau driven by a gaily-attired coachman?

In holding such absurd notions the native is simply worshipping at the altar of the great god "humbug," whose cult is not unknown further west, and let us trust that he may soon turn from so vain an idol.

But enough as to the native legal practitioner and his mistaken ideas, and let us turn to the pleasanter subject of the English barrister, your rival and friend. And here at once the new-comer finds a hearty welcome and genuine kindness. The senior members, with well-appointed houses, invite him to their hospitable entertainments, the juniors put him up for the local club, or help him to purchase pony trap or dog cart, and protect his "griff" ignorance from being imposed upon.

Oh, the pleasant hours spent with my brethren of the long-robe! Oh, the pleasant and witty chats in the bar library; the *repartee* keen but courteous; the help and advice given freely and ungrudgingly!

> "My life is full of weary days,
> But good things have not kept aloof."

And amongst my pleasantest memories I treasure the Bar association in Allahabad.

This seems a suitable place for discussing what incomes are to be made up country; as compared to the enormous sums realized in Calcutta and Bombay they will sound small. The three largest incomes (so far as I know) made by men of fifteen years' standing all exceed £5,000 a year. Then might be placed half-a-dozen ranging from £3,000 to £1,500; and below this the strugglers! Life is dear in India, and a barrister cannot live the pleasant, inexpensive life of a subaltern. Oh, dear no, he must impress the native mind with an appearance of wealth if he would hope to get good fees, and a man making £700 a year will not save much of it against that rainy day we pensionless ones ought to dread and provide for. Those before alluded to who try their fortune away from High Courts must be contented with a maximum of £1,500 a year; but as a set off their expenses are far less.

How nice these various incomes sound to the ear of briefless at home; but *audi alteram partem;* you will make a nice income so long only as your health allows you to work hard, but not a day longer. Work hard, begin to feel the joy of success, break down and be ordered home to save your life—hard lines, very hard lines will you find them. Should you recover sufficiently to try India again you will have to begin at the bottom of the ladder, as native clients are fickle, and absence by no means causes their hearts to get fonder. Life in India to the man in health is a good thing, the work is hard and the play is hard, but the slackness induced by fever and liver soon produce a piteous change.

I remember, as if it were yesterday, the light-heartedness with which, in my second year, I accepted a case which necessitated riding twenty-four miles to a Magistrate's camp, working from 10 a.m. to 5 p.m., and then twenty-four miles home (there was a dance that evening, and we kept it up pretty late); had I been offered such a programme a few years later it would have been impossible for me to accept it even without the frivolous ending.

May I venture on a word of advice. If you are prepared to work hard, nay, harder than the successful counsel in London, and can afford to wait five or six years, stay in one of the presidency towns, Calcutta, Bombay, or Madras. Success there is worth having. And should health fail you there is more chance of getting into a Privy Council practice at home than if you hail from less exalted places.

Only to think of some who spend six months in Calcutta and six in London making £20,000 a year is enough to make one break the whole ten commandments; but such exist—go and do thou likewise.

The natives are pressing us hard, every year the struggle becomes fiercer. If the learned old Vakil is not so often met with, the smart young native who has been to England and rubbed off his Oriental courtesy against the very bourgeois society alone open to him in London abounds. Such a youth will, if encouraged, produce photos of "the girl he left behind him," and affect the Don Juan. Luckless milliner or shop "lidy" who fondly believed an Indian Prince had come a-courting!

Curse all the nonsense talked about inter-marriage of the East and West! I agree with a ribald friend of mine, who had for half-an-hour stood the ravings of a native gentleman advocating free inter-marriage of the English with their Aryan brethren. "What!" he exclaimed, for the twentieth time, "what would be the result if I, who belong to one of the most ancient families in Asia, were to marry an English lady?"

"Do you want an answer?" quoth R. F. The oldest blood in Asia bowed. "Well, the natural result would be black and tan." Oh, Lord, how could he have said it? But, all the same, learn, oh, olive-tinted offspring of all the ages, that the women of England, down to the smallest kitchen wench, are beyond your reach so long as manhood and chivalry thrive in the old country.

Free your own women from their hideous bondage ere you come snivelling around our daughters; perchance, when free, your home-growth will surprise you.

I myself have seen some of these so-called "curry and rice" marriages, which without being openly unhappy, yet filled one with a great pity for the misguided woman.

However educated and advanced her husband may be, the whole turn and bent of his mind will be at variance with the ideas which come naturally to a decent English woman; the ordinary respect shown by us to womankind in her person will fill his Eastern mind with jealous alarm.

Then only imagine the feelings of a white mother whose children, instead of being delicately olive-tinted, throw back to some objectionable ancestor, and appear as black as her boot!

But stay, O babbling brook, dry up, I pray thee, or at least flow orderly in your appointed channel.

Having located our barrister and warned him to play as hard as he can, let us visit him in chambers.

It takes some time to learn whether the various clients who besiege your office from early dawn are really thinking of engaging your professional services, or only trying to get an opinion for nothing. The latter class are very numerous, and not easy to deal with, as every man with a case is at liberty to walk round where he pleases and request each limb of the law to read and give an opinion as to the result of the litigation. No fee for reading documents? Oh, dear me, no! If you don't care to examine his case the gentleman can go elsewhere. A smart Munshi is invaluable in helping to sort the sheep from the goats, but smart Munshis do not grow on every cactus hedge, and you will soon learn to depend on your own judgment of a client's worth and intentions.

Then, again, the personal appearance of constituents must not deceive you. Here is a haughty-looking swell with a gorgeous puggari and garments of great magnificence, there a distinctly dirty, meanly-attired personage, the former evidently conferring honour by his presence, the latter well-nigh apologising for the trouble he causes; nevertheless the former is a ruined Mahomedan whose worldly wealth is on his back, and the latter one of the richest "Mahajans" (bankers) in the district.

I have known clients who deemed it wise to array themselves in rags when about to visit their legal adviser so as to impress him with their utter inability to pay proper fees, but this is too shallow a device to avail them long. The fees for civil suits are fixed by law, but in criminal cases counsel make their own terms.

Let us suppose for a moment that the terms are agreed upon, what next? Something very important, and never to be neglected. Get your fee to its last anna into your own hands, as numberless are the devices to keep back some part, however small, of the amount due; if careless about this you simply open the door to "Dalali" (brokerage) and other kinds of roguery.

I have seen a bag containing Rs. 999 lying on the table, the case called on, and counsel refuse to move till the one rupee still due was produced.

Being then a beginner I thought this harsh, but soon learnt that in the best interests of the Bar he could not have acted otherwise; if A allows one rupee to be kept back then B can overlook ten, and the old "Dusturi" game begins again.

Of course when engaged in a case likely to last some time, you must secure the fee for several days in advance, and be careful not to let your work done outrun its remuneration, as to get payment afterwards is well-nigh a hopeless job.

This direct dealing with filthy lucre is not pleasant for a man whose profession bids him treat fees, not as payment for his services, but as the free gift of grateful clients, but unless he pockets his pride and takes the money due in a firm grip he will be helping swindling in many forms too numerous to detail here.

Well, I know that the sort of fee-thieves I have been alluding to are also to be found in England, as, for instance, the solicitor who marks fifty guineas on a brief and pays twenty-five, promising the remainder shortly!

So much for clients and their fees, and now we will turn with due reverence to all the powers that be, magistrates, deputy magistrates, collectors, assistant collectors, commissioners, deputy commissioners, high court judges, district judges, subordinate judges *et hoc genus omne*, before whom a barrister appears in India, and for the sake of brevity let us call them all judges.

Judges are, I believe, fairly plentiful in America, but the race thrives well in India, and to write a learned disquisition on the various species of the genus judge might be of interest to students of human nature in all its forms and aspects, studies under such headings as the learned judge, the courteous judge, the irascible judge, the native loving, the "nigger" hating, the "don't care a tinker's malediction for forms and procedure" judge, might be made and illustrated with pen and ink sketches life size. But all such splitting up of the question would not advance us much.

In the course of my narrative two kinds alone come into play: First, the one who would listen, and second, the one who would not. Personally I prefer the former.

Cleverness, quickness of perception, good memory, courteous manners, may all come under the head of "circumstances over which one has no control," but the dullest man can listen, and when the liberty, nay, perchance, the life of a fellow being is at stake, is it too much to expect from his judge that he will carefully listen to the voice of the accused speaking through his counsel?

There is no doubt that the habit of ignorant and impertinent native legal practitioners, who avail themselves of every opportunity to inflict bombastic and nonsensical speeches on the bench, has to some extent caused their victims to retaliate by writing the decision before coming to court.

I once had to appear before a Sessions Judge who was notoriously deaf to argument; my clients were charged with riot and robbery, and twenty-two witnesses for the Crown gave promise of a long trial. Before the case began I was called into the room behind the court and welcomed as follows: "No need to trouble yourself, my dear fellow, as I have determined to acquit your clients."

After this there was nothing more for me

to do but to sit still and listen to the judge ballyragging witnesses for the Crown in a way that speedily caused a total collapse.

As it turned out all went well and we parted good friends, but had it been my duty on that day to appear for the prosecution things would have become lively. What especially amused me was that my clients were really guilty, and fully expected punishment.

Now this worthy man who considered half-an-hour spent in listening as a terrible waste of time, had spent several hours in reading up the police papers and the record generally, only to arrive at a wrong result.

It was the greater pity as he was undoubtedly a very able man, a splendid linguist, and a thorough sportsman, but we all have our little failings.

I remember, however, one dear old fossil, who ought to have been shelved long ago, and he listened too much; first one side convinced him and then the other. The only thing to do was to hand him up the notes of one's argument to peruse at his leisure, they were faithfully transmitted into his judgment.

The advice of Polonius might well be taken to heart by some of our worthy Daniels.

"Give every man thine ear, but few thy voice," and yet the most talkative of them may well plead that he is only imitating in a humble and imperfect manner the example of more than one judge of the High Court, which is to him even as a beacon set upon a hill. But hush, I blaspheme. "Muaf kyjye."

One word here to my future brethren of the Bar; be not extreme to mark what is amiss; a hasty word, a slight discourtesy from an over-worked man, with, perchance, a liver, can well be met with gentleness; deliberate rudeness will rarely come in your way, but should it do so the remedy is easy to find.

Whichever Bar Association you may belong to can at any time protect its members by representation to the High Court, which, of course, comes with far greater force than any individual action. But somehow, the best class of barristers rarely, if ever, fall foul of the judges.

The narrow limits of an Indian social circle naturally bring Bench and Bar into greater intimacy than is altogether desirable; it is not always pleasant to argue a case before a man you are on very familiar terms with, nor is a tiff over whist or angry words over a disputed dance the best preparation for an impartial hearing.

A luckless friend of mine who resided in a station whereof the society amounted to eighteen souls only, managed to fall foul of the Collector Sahib, who made things lively for him; sent to Coventry, boycotted, severely left alone was he until a year later another Pharaoh arose, and my poor friend was once more smiled upon.

The few civilians now remaining who can say "I was at Haileybury and am not a 'competition wallah,'" are the pleasantest to meet; with them you are sure of courteous treatment, which is more than an uncertainty with some of the productions of cram and competition.

A little story to illustrate the different men.

In a large town not far from the Taj, the Hindus love not the Mahomedans, and the latter return the compliment with interest; now every few years it comes to pass that a Hindu festival, whereat much laughter and joy is needed, coincides with the Mussulman "Mohurrum," saddest of all fast days, whence arise ructions that would do honour to an Irish election.

Some ten years ago I, on behalf of the Hindus, presented a petition to tho then Collector, praying that the Mussulman leaders should be bound over to keep the peace; a similar petition was handed in by counsel for the Mahomedans. An old hand this Collector, and fond of his joke. "Gentlemen," he said, "the festivals are this day week at ten o'clock, and the point of friction, if any, must be the open space in front of the Kotwali; we will therefore adjourn the hearing of this case till then; instead of gowns, let me suggest breeches and boots!"

A week later I rode down to the place indicated, to find the Collector Sahib Bahadur mounted on a big handsome waler, with half-a-dozen policemen and the Kotwal. The two processions passed, not a dog wagged his tail, and the town resumed its usual sleepy condition. Four years later—the Collector being no longer my old Bahadur friend, but a very learned man, quite the Pundit—a similar state of things arose.

First of all he pooh-poohed the pleaders out of Court; they, naturally resenting this, applied to the High Court, who promptly combed his locks. Alarmed, he now heard everyone and everything for hours on end, and as the eventful day approached gave such wonderful orders as to the processions that a first-class riot ensued, and the military had to be called out.

The native of India is not unlike the horse, in that he soon knows whether his rider is afraid of him or not. He needs the Bahadur, not the Pundit.

A fine specimen of the former class was a certain well-known Cantonment Magistrate, the best of good fellows, but with sounder notions upon practical justice than on legal procedure.

His idea of a sentence was that the sooner it was executed the better, and, consequently, after having listened with exemplary patience to the vapid raving of a Bengali pleader, who fondly imagined he was eloquently defending the prisoner, he said —

"Finding guilty, I sentence to fifteen cuts with a cane."

Whereupon the Bengali —

"Oh, sir, my lord, I should like to appeal

against the sentence. May I have a copy of the judgment ?"

"Certainly," said the courteous Magistrate, but even as he spoke cries of distress from the yard behind the Court proved beyond all doubt that the fifteen cuts were being vigorously applied.

In vain the Babu reiterated —

"I want to appeal! I want to appeal!" but the music from the compound continued *molto crescendo.*

Good old Major, how the natives feared you! How clean they kept every bazaar and gully along which your keen eye was likely to travel. No mobbing or beating European soldiers heard of in our cantonments. Tommy himself the while knows better than to play the goat within reach of your tender mercies.

If ever these lines meet the eye of the judge to whom I am about to refer I trust he will accept my respectful admiration for his conduct of the case, and for the extreme tact and courtesy he then manifested to my colleague, Mr. Beddy, and myself.

We had to defend the "Gomashta" or agent of a wealthy firm, accused of having embezzled Rs. 60,000!

The junior partner conducted the prosecution, aided by several slippery Vakils.

Our instructions were that the missing monies had been skilfully misappropriated to his private account by the actual prosecutor, in a series of fraudulent entries, extending over three years.

Now, though good all round, Beddy was pre-eminent in dealing with native account-books, hence I took the part of a lay figure in the following proceedings.

First of all we obtained from the Court a day's adjournment to inspect the voluminous accounts, and spent many hours tracing with the help of our client the course of the fraud.

Before commencing the trial the judge asked us, Were we really going to call the long list of witnesses which some wretched pleader had supplied ?

"Not one of them," said Beddy, laughing, "if you will promise to let me cross-examine the prosecutor to my heart's content."

"So you shall, Mr. Beddy, as you are not one to waste the time of the Court," was the prompt reply.

Strong in this assurance, my old friend went to work, cross-examined the luckless prosecutor from ten till four on five consecutive days, with this startling result, that the accused and the prosecutor changed places, a little game of post which eventually cost the latter some years' rigorous imprisonment.

During all these five days the judge toiled on patiently, never interrupting unnecessarily, but keeping an intelligent grip on the case from start to finish.

It must have been on one of the evenings of this trial that old Mr. Beddy gave me a sketch of his life.

As a lad of seventeen he had persuaded his father to let him start from home with an available capital of Rs. 100. By hook or by crook he picked up some knowledge of engineering, and found employment in some bridge building operations. A bad fall brought him down to very low straits, and as he himself said, many a day a handful of parched peas was all he had to stay his hunger.

Fortune, however, turned her wheel and smiled on the lad, who would rather starve than be a burden on his parents, and for many years Beddy was engaged as a land agent.

Having in this capacity to attend the Sudder Diwani Court, where a case of his employer's was being argued, Beddy found to his disgust that it was going against him, because none of his counsel had grasped the right point in dispute.

At length his hot Irish blood asserted itself, and jumping up in Court he exclaimed in stentorian tones, "Will your lordships hear me before deciding the case?"

Highly irregular and most reprehensible, no doubt, but a good-natured bench heard him, and were so impressed that they decided the case in his favour, one of them remarking that though no pleader, Mr. Beddy was a sound lawyer.

Encouraged by this success he soon after qualified, and in the days I speak of no criminal in the N.W.P. thought himself properly defended unless Beddy Sahib stood by him.

Alas, his massive form and ragged, unkempt beard, his keen but kindly eyes will no more be seen in the various Mufassal Courts!

After a long life of hard work the old pleader rests in the Agra churchyard.

One more specimen, "Punctuality Jim," or "Old Punctuality," as he was generally termed. Nice old party this, with a creed not unlike bad language which ran thus:

"I believe in myself and in no one else; also that time was made for slaves; furthermore that High Courts are inventions of the devil, and that barristers will perish eternally! Amen."

This aged Solomon lived in a well-nigh inaccessible district, and went to Court or not just as the fancy took him; pleasant for a barrister who had travelled night and day to attend on some fixed date, and who wanted to get back as soon as possible.

In vain the High Court remonstrated, "Gallio cared for none of these things."

Retribution overtook him at the hands of a cheeky young limb of the law, who punctually at ten a.m. entered the empty Court, whence he despatched a telegram to the Registrar in Allahabad, politely forwarding a copy to "Old P." No result!

Half-an-hour more, another telegram to headquarters, another copy for information.

Towards mid-day the Judge appeared in a fury, but soon found it safer to vent his wrath on Sherishtadars and Chuprassis than on the long robe, and being fairly collared, played the game according to book. Very different was the conduct of "Shekari Bill," who bade you fix your own time, provided only you arranged matters so as to stay dinner, where good food and better drink awaited your arrival.

CHAPTER III.

In spite of my promise, made at the outset, to avoid legal "shop," a few incidents from the lighter side of Court life may perhaps be excused. It must be remembered that most of the events related took place in small Mufassal Courts, where, although cases are conducted with all order and decency, yet a greater latitude is allowed to both sides than would be tolerated in a High Court, and further in such places counsel must often step across and ask the prisoner for information if he finds him intelligent, as the local pleaders may be worse than useless. With these words of apologetic explanation I proceed to spin my yarns.

"THE VOICE OF CONSCIENCE."

"Oh, coward conscience, how dost thou afflict me!"
Richard III., Act v., Scene 2.

An amusing incident happened to me some years ago, whilst defending a rich Zemindar, implicated with five or six others (for whom I did not appear) in a charge of murder.

The evidence against my client was of the weakest, except for the confession of a co-accused, which certainly made it appear that my client was the *fons et origo mali.*

Such a piece of evidence could not be dealt with lightly, and, to make matters worse, the Sessions Judge, before whom the case came for trial, was notoriously of the hanging order. In the thirty-seven cases which had preceded the trial I am speaking of he had convicted thirty-six times!

The accused men stood side by side at the back of the Court, and accidentally my client was next to the man whose evidence told so strongly against him.

Having need of some information, I left my seat and went over to the dock.

My client told me what I wanted, but as I was turning away he said in a somewhat trembling voice —

"Alas, Sahib, things look bad. Shall I ever again be restored to my children?"

The grief of the old man, contrasting as it did with the smug satisfaction painted on the Judas' face beside him, fairly angered me, and I said to him, not without several strong words in Hindustani —

"Be calm, the justice of the Sirkar will not fail you, but you will yet see that son of a dog beside you swinging high in the air."

I regained my seat, and the trial proceeded.

About five minutes later a wild, unearthly yell arose from the dock —

"Boo-hoo! boo-hoo-oo-oo-oo!" *ad infinitum.*

The Judge scowled, the Court officials shrieked "Chupraho" till they were hoarse.

Looking round to see the cause of all this hubbub, I discovered that it came from my friend Judas, who, with both hands raised to heaven, was vociferating—

"I don't want to be hung! I don't want to be hung! I'll tell the truth if you won't hang me!"

The Judge, in a most tremendous rage, ordered two constables to bundle him out of Court, whereupon I intervened and suggested to his Honour that what we were now hearing must be the voice of conscience.

The next ten minutes were spent in a somewhat unpleasant wrangle, but I gained my point, and Judas was brought forward and asked what he wanted, and why he was howling.

His reply was somewhat startling—

"I never saw the murder committed. I am quite innocent, but that policeman there promised to get me ten rupees if I gave evidence in this case. He taught me word by word, and letter by letter. And now why should I be hanged? Boo-hoo! boo-hoo!"

His agonizing howls again rose loud and clear.

It was delicious to see the Judge quieting and comforting the miserable wretch.

Of course my client was acquitted, and the evidence of the victim of conscience brought several police officers to well-merited punishment.

The following story is a somewhat striking illustration of how little reliance can be placed in India upon evidence of identification.

In a village near Futehghur lived a wealthy old Thakur, who had an only son.

This young fellow had for some time been carrying on an intrigue with the wife of a Brahmin, and consequently one fine morning, when the husband disappeared, suspicion fastened upon the Lovelace, and when a few days later a corpse was found which the guilty lady herself declared to be that of her missing husband, which her father-in-law swore to be that of his son, and which half-a-dozen neighbours recognized beyond all doubt, the suspicion became so strong that after due process of the law he stood before the Judge at Sessions charged with murder.

I was for the defence, and on the second day of the trial was cross-examining the Brahmin fair—cause of all this trouble—when suddenly she threw up her hands and screamed, whereupon a man from amongst the crowd in Court came forward and proceeded to console her.

Who was it? Why, her husband, alive and well!

It seems that after a quarrel with his wife he had shouldered his beggar's wallet and gone for a small pilgrimage to Muttra, whence he had only just returned.

He seemed to think it a magnificent joke that the body found should have been taken for his, the moral of which story is: Do not try to identify a corpse which has been three days exposed to an Indian sun.

> "How monstrous
> It was . . .
> To kill their gracious father!"
>
> *Macbeth.*

> "As true as it is strange,
> For truth is truth
> To the end of reckoning."
>
> *Measure for Measure.*

"If you wish me to defend your relatives successfully tell me the truth. Why try to deceive me, who am your friend? If I cannot believe that your adversaries murdered their own father, and accused your side of having done it, how much less will the Judge believe such a story?"

I spoke strongly, nay, even angrily, and the eight or ten men who sat around me on the ground looked up with eyes full of reproach, and, I may almost say, distrust.

At length an elderly Thakur, the brother of the accused, stood up and came close to my chair.

"Sahib," he said, and his voice trembled with emotion, "try and forget that you are a white man, and look on this through my eyes, though I am but your slave. You white men do not know what hatred means —a hatred which father bequeaths to son, and son to grandson—a hatred to gratify which each member of the family would gladly die. This is what we mean by our hatred, and in the light of these words listen to what I say.

"By the holy waters of the Ganges, by the life of my son, what I now tell you is truth. I saw it with my eyes. I heard it with my ears.

"My brother, Ram Singh, and his four sons were going to their field work, and on the way, about two hundred paces from the village, they met Attar Singh and his two sons, and his two nephews. Since long a bitter feud has existed between these two families. Abuse passed between them, and finally blows were struck. Attar Singh himself struck the first blow, whereupon Ram Singh and his sons, who are all good men and tall, raised their latties (bamboo clubs) and used them so effectually that their opponents fled before them. At the door of Attar Singh's home lay his old father, ninety years of age, blind and unable to move. After some discussion, the party who had run away raised this old man up in their arms and carried him back to where the fight had been" (Ram Singh and his party had passed on to their work). "Arrived at the place, Attar Singh struck the old father a lattie blow on his head. The skull was broken, and the feeble flame of life flickered and went out. Then Attar Singh cried aloud and said, 'See, all men, what Ram Singh and his sons have done! They have killed my father, and beaten me!' Whereupon he sent a man to run swiftly to the nearest Thanah, and when the police came he reported fully that Ram Singh and his sons had waylaid and beaten him and killed his father. Then came the Thanadar and held an investigation. Attar Singh is rich, Ram Singh is poor, and the police have reported in favour of Attar Singh, so that now my brother and his sons are accused of murder, and unless your Honour can save them their lives will be forfeited. But, be the result what it may, I have told nothing but the truth to the Sahib."

I sat for some time almost stupefied; the old man's manner and simple eloquent words had made a strange impression on me. But what a story to tell in Court!

What a defence to raise before the old and experienced civilian Judge, who was to try the case the next day.

At length I said: "My friends, you must trust me entirely; I shall endeavour by my cross-examination to shake the story for the prosecution so completely that it will not be necessary for us to make such defence. Your witnesses will, however, be in attendance, and *Jo hoga, so hoga, Kismet ke-hat hai.*" (What will be will be, the matter is Kismet.)

The old man who had previously spoken said, "It is good, and we trust you, but the witnesses for the prosecution have been well trained, the Thanadar himself taught them what to say."

The men departed, leaving me to think over the position, which certainly did not seem smiling. Experience had taught me that however much I might trip up witnesses for the Crown, yet if cleverly trained they would stick to the main points of their story well enough to secure a conviction, the more so if I ventured upon such an extraordinary defence as the one suggested above.

At six o'clock the next morning the case began, and witness after witness glibly told the story of how Attar Singh and his old father had been set upon by Ram Singh and his four sons, who had killed the old man and beaten his son.

I was in despair; my cross-examination had not materially shaken the first three witnesses. The fourth witness was beginning his story—"I was in my field at work—"

I turned to my notes; the third witness had began his evidence, "I was in my field at work," so had the second, so had the first; there were ten witnesses, each one of them began his evidence in a similar way.

I breathed again and rushed out of Court. My old friend the Thakur quickly rejoined me.

"Where is your Putwarri?" (village official, accountant and surveyor).

"Here he is, Sahib."

"Has he his map of the village fields?"

"Yes, here it is."

From his dictation I took down the numbers of the fields surrounding the scene of the murder, and got back into Court just in time to ask the Judge to kindly recall all the witnesses, and ask each of them the number of his field. I rapidly explained to him in English what I had obtained from the Putwarri, and how I hoped to show that if the men were, as they said, working in their fields, it must have been impossible for them to have seen anything of the alleged murder—nay, more, that some of these witnesses who pretended to be working in their fields had no land at all and belonged to a neighbouring village. The Government pleader, a fat and impertinent Bengāli Bābu, began to jabber some nonsense about the irregularity of my proceedings, but he had to do with a Judge whose one wish was to get at the truth, however that might best be done, and his objections were soon swept aside.

Oh, the faces of the witnesses as they were recalled and asked, "What is the number of your field?" No more was necessary, as the Putwarri's map and evidence did the rest. I could see that the Judge took a very different view of the case from what he had been inclined to do at first, and when at length I got the fat Thanadar into the witness box and cross-examined him for three hours the case for the Crown began to look fishy.

At a hint from the Judge, though sorely against my will, the defence was now begun, and the same story which the old Thakur had told me was sworn to by several witnesses.

I watched the Judge's face as the extraordinary account of how Attar Singh committed parricide was unfolded, and thanked my stars that my clients did not only depend on such a defence, as he evidently did not believe one word of it, and in fact, when the trial was over, he told me that after twenty-five years of experience he had never heard such an improbable story.

My clients were acquitted, and the Thanadar and the ten witnesses eventually brought to punishment.

My old Thakur friend sends me once a

year a bottle of home-made rose water, and whenever I meet him solemnly adheres to the truth of the story he told me above.

Subsequently I told the story to several of my native friends, and found that to their minds there was nothing in it impossible or even improbable.

Many of them indeed capped it with stories from their personal experience, full of such deadly hatred and vengeance that not for the first time I was left in wonder at the gentle ways of the mild Hindu.

> "There was nothing lying at my foot
> But lifeless flesh and bone!"
>
> HOOD.

Considering how many more dogs there are than bones, it is indeed lucky that the tastes of my learned brethren differ so widely. One barrister doggie's meat is another's poison, which premises being admitted I venture to confess my special preference. Let others enjoy a stiff will, a knotty point in conveyancing, a sweet thing in libel, or a racy divorce, but give me a good murder!

There is an excitement in defending a man accused of this crime, a breathless anxiety from start to finish, a feeling that a human life depends on your words, which never seem so keen in other cases and at other times.

You know your man is innocent. Of course you do, or a fine counsel you must be! The Crown is hounding on its police bloodhounds, and you alone with the help of the worthy jury can save the accused! The Judge—did you say the Judge? Bless your innocence, the Judge, if he rightly understands his business, only comes in at the end of the trial, and does the ornamental! If he gets interfering too soon he must be sat on, to which laudable end the prosecuting counsel will generally lend a hand!

In India murder cases are pretty plentiful and lead to nice heavy fees, but, thank goodness, it is not often that one Englishman stands accused of killing another, and great was the excitement in Agra when it became known that a Corporal in the R.A. had been foully murdered as he was walking along with his wife. When, however, the wife and a Sergeant in the same battery were arrested and made over to the civil power the cackling became portentous.

It seems that the accused persons had been carrying on an intrigue for some time past, and that the murdered man had objected strongly on several occasions to their intimacy. On the evening of the murder, at twenty minutes to nine, the Corporal and his wife left the barracks together, and were seen to turn into the road which crosses the parade ground, skirts the front of the cemetery, and leads up to three bungalows occupied by pensioners. At one of these houses the luckless man had promised to pay a visit, but, after hearing the gun fired at 9 p.m., the expectant host concluded his guests were not coming, and proceeded to turn in. A few minutes later the Corporal's wife rushed in, exclaiming "Come quick, a man in a red puggari has killed my husband. He struck him with a tent peg!" Now, considering the night was pitch dark the wife's words are terribly suggestive of foreknowledge! The old pensioner with a servant promptly lit a lantern and accompanied the woman to the cemetery corner, where the poor fellow lay stone dead. One blow behind the left ear had sufficed, and a large tent peg stained with blood lay close at hand, giving a terrible import to the woman's words.

More help soon came, and the body was taken to the military hospital. Several gunners, hearing what had happened, hurried round, and four of them carried their comrade to a couch. One of these four was the Sergeant! Does a murderer generally hasten to come face to face with his victim?

Early next morning the Major commanding the battery, accompanied by the

Cantonment Magistrate and the District Superintendent of Police, searched the Sergeant's room. They found him hard at work—washing a pair of kharki trousers, the said garments being much stained—blood-stained!

Evidence was adduced to prove that the Sergeant was in his room at fourteen minutes to nine on the night in question.

Three witnesses proved this. One of them, the Sergeant-Major, had looked at his watch, and the prosecution admitted this as proved. But no one saw the accused from fourteen minutes to nine till a quarter-past nine, when he entered the Sergeants' mess and joined in a game of whist. This last time was not disputed by the Crown, as a large clock faced the players.

The theory of the prosecution was that, acting in concert with her lover, the wife had detained her husband till dark, had then started at a pre-arranged time and gone by a certain road. That by a short cut across the plain the murderer could easily get to the cemetery corner before his victim passed, whence, springing out, he dealt the fatal blow, and then rushed back in time to join the whist players at 9.15 !

Now, like all theories for the prosecution, this sounds plausible till carefully dissected. And first of all we must remember it was the merry month of May in the plains of India! If you run ten yards you perspire! If you run for twenty minutes and survive it you will at least show signs of the effort undergone. Now the men who saw the accused at 9.15 all swore he was cool and calm till the news came that the Corporal was being carried in badly hurt, when he, like the others, got excited and rushed off to the hospital, where we have seen him.

When defending this part of the case it became important for me to find out how swiftly a good runner might travel from the Royal Artillery Barracks along the Kutcha Lane across to the cemetery corner, and back again. I offered a rupee to whichever of my Syces did the best time, and rode with them to see fair play. The winner did the distance in twenty-seven minutes, which would have left him two minutes for the murder. But surely if a trained native runner took twenty-seven minutes in broad daylight, when he could see the goal all the time, it is too much to pretend that the murderer plunging along on a pitch dark night could travel as fast.

In the Magistrates' Court the accused were defended by a pleader, Mr. Beddy, to my mind the cleverest hand at cross-examining in India. To hear him turn native witnesses inside out was a treat!

Despite a very rough exterior Beddy was a very gentle, easy-going man, who hated any unpleasantness with the Bench, and great was my surprise when he rushed into my chambers and entreated me to come and help him to defend the Sergeant! It seems the Magistrate had recorded the evidence at his sweet will and pleasure, and been rude to my old friend when remonstrated with.

I hurried into Court and found things very bad. Never have I seen evidence so scandalously treated. Three times in the first ten minutes did we have to pull him up, and then I lost my temper and gave it him hot. Things grew lively, but the evidence was taken down correctly. Some forty witnesses were examined, and both the accused were committed for trial to the High Court at Allahabad.

When the day came the Court was terribly crowded; ladies even and heads of departments struggled for seats, whilst behind them Tommy Atkins in hundreds determined to hear all, the Sergeant looking smart and soldierly, despite his long imprisonment; the female accused, dark and repulsive, but strangely calm and indifferent.

What a splendid witness the British officer is! Yes! No! I do not know! He tells the truth and nothing but the truth.

As a set-off, however, we had several talkative female witnesses, one of whom gave me a terrible fall. She was the belle of the battery, and we had acted together in a burlesque some few months before, consequently when down at barracks collecting evidence and measuring distances this fair lady had walked about with me—this by way of explanation. Imagine my feelings when in answer to my first question, "How far is it from your quarters to the canteen?" she replied, "Well, sir, seeing as how the werry last time I walked from our quarters to the canteen you was walking beside me, perhaps you will answer that question yourself!"

Tableau! So much for being solicitor as well as counsel.

We were also treated to the young medical witness, who is cocksure of all he says, and thinks no one but a doctor can understand his evidence. He was to prove that six months before his death the luckless Corporal was in hospital suffering from ague fever, that his wife brought him tea at four o'clock every day, that one night the patient was taken ill, and the symptoms then shown pointed to arsenical poisoning! I shall never regret the dressing I gave this youth.

He had not at the time reported the matter, or made any note thereof; he had not found arsenic, nor indeed taken any steps for such search; he had not warned the man that an attempt had been made to poison him; and finally, when confronted with some well-known medical works, was forced to admit that the symptoms he had detailed were all to be expected in the course of a bad ague fever. Fancy swearing a life away in so reckless a fashion!

For five long weary days the stream of witnesses flowed on, and then came the defence; witnesses to prove that three days before the murder the Sergeant had been out shooting, and that in cutting the throat of a black buck the kharki trousers he was wearing had been splashed and stained; witnesses to prove the exact distance from the barracks to the cemetery and back; witnesses to subsequent conduct; and finally witnesses to character.

The jury retire, and being good men and true, promptly say not guilty!

On the second day of the trial, having noticed a very charming friend listening to the proceedings with much interest, I ventured to ask her had she formed any opinion as to the guilt or innocence of the accused?

"Oh, dear me, yes; there cannot be a doubt on the subject," she said. "The Sergeant must be innocent, because he is so good-looking; but the woman knows all about it."

And yet there are wretches who say women ought not to serve on juries! Nearly two months after the trial the lady who has hitherto figured as the accused honoured me with a visit.

"She was pretty well, thank you, despite the unfeeling conduct of her late husband!"

I began to feel creepy.

"What does he do?"

"Well, not much, but he looks over my shoulder when I comb out my hair! *Br-r-r! Qy hai! brandy peg, jaldi lao!*"

FALSTAFF:—"As I was then advised by my learned counsel in the laws of this land's service, I did not come."

A frivolous friend of mine, also a barrister, got into a nice scrape and got out of it again in a way that was more amusing than correct. He was one day waiting in the verandah outside the Magistrates' Court when he noticed that a tall Police Sowar had planted himself a few feet off, and was staring with all his eyes; now, though a cat may look at a king, a native of India ought not to stare at an Englishman, not that there is any law against it, but by doing so he proclaims the fact that he wishes to be impertinent.

Had my friend been longer in the country he would either have taken no notice or have said two words which would have brought the tears into the man's eyes and turned his liver to water, but unfortunately he pursued neither of these courses, and instead, sharply asked the man why he stared at him.

The scamp replied, "Because it is my pleasure," a reply which promptly obtained for him the order of the boot.

The fat was now in the fire, and the Sowar loudly proclaimed his intention of lodging a complaint.

"I'll help you," said my friend, and seizing him by the scruff of the neck he landed him with a well-planted kick into the awful presence of the Collector Sahib Bahadhur!

No words of mine could express the rage of the noble Magistrate, but as Bon Gaultier would say —

> "The collector smiled, with frenzy wild his very beard waxed blue,
> His shirt it could not hold him, so wrathy riled he grew."

By-the-bye, blue is not the right colour; red would be truer to life, but does not suit the verse.

A summons against the "Ballister Sahib," as natives always call us, was promptly made out, and the case set down for hearing.

The same evening this learned and worthy Magistrate betook himself to the local club, and there in the presence of two officers announced in the most pompous tones that he meant to make it hot for young Mr. C—.

"I'll just cool his blood with a few hours' confinement. A fine won't do."

This and much more in the same style.

Knowing that I was engaged to defend C—, the two gentlemen I have referred to came and told me all that had been said, and allowed me to make a note of it with a view to drawing up affidavits if necessary.

On the day fixed for hearing the case I appeared before the fiery Magistrate and told him that I had a preliminary objection to offer. He made some very rude remarks about trusting that I was not going to waste the time of the Court with "any puerile technicalities." I smiled blandly, and assured him that I was too well aware how valuable his time was to wish to waste any of it, but that as he had already openly prejudged the case he could no longer try it, and explained what I have referred to above.

He tried to make light of it, and declared he would go on with the case. I handed in a telegram to be at once sent to the High Court if he persisted. It was worded as follows:—

"Mag. and Col. X. before hearing any evidence has openly declared sentence he intends passing. Affidavits follow."

He did not like it, but after some hesitation decided to send the case to another Magistrate.

So far so good, but my friend C— had a very smart bearer, who came to him about this time with a mysterious demand for

Rs. 10, which when given him caused him to smile sweetly.

When next seen the bearer and the complainant Sowar were on the most friendly terms.

Can this account for the fact that on the day of trial the complainant failed to recognize his assailant, etc., etc., etc.?

Alas for Indian veracity!

A CLOSE SHAVE.

One morning very early, when about to start for my ride, I suddenly found myself in the embraces of a native woman! Be not shocked, gentle reader, for her embraces were confined entirely to my riding boots.

Of course I at once knew that only some very powerful motive could have driven her to behave in such an unseemly manner, and so it proved.

"My husband, who is innocent, is to be hanged unless your Honour will save him?"

"What is he accused of?"

"He is falsely accused of having murdered a dancing girl. She was last seen alive in the ekka of which he was the driver."

Now it may be prejudice on my part, or it may be a sort of kink in my mind due to an over-fondness for French novels of the Gaboriau style, but I certainly have a weakness for the luckless man who was last seen in company of a person subsequently found murdered, and the poor woman's story interested me.

Her husband had been sentenced to death in Saharanpur, and the case had, as usual, been sent up to the High Court for confirmation of sentence.

How this poor penniless creature had managed to find her way such a distance, and why she applied to me for help and sympathy will ever be a mystery to me.

I promised to read through the record of her husband's case and see if I could find anything to urge on his behalf, and in fulfilment of this promise found myself toiling through a heavy criminal file.

The language of the judgment struck me at once as painfully flippant, and, indeed, as the poor fellow had not been defended, some strange liberties had been taken.

The case was down for hearing on the next day, but the good-natured Chief Justice adjourned it for a week at my request, with leave to have all the police papers translated.

Now the first rock ahead was that the accused had made a full confession before the committing Magistrate, which, however, he had repudiated before the Sessions Judge, alleging that it had been extracted from him by torture.

Would you know how he was tortured?

By being kept awake for eight consecutive days and nights—nothing more! Conceive to yourself what this means in the plains of India.

A drop of red pepper in his eye and a few

prods from the policeman's bayonet did all that was needed.

He would have confessed to every crime in the decalogue to obtain a few hours' sleep.

But I have anticipated here what the poor wretch subsequently told me, and as it would be useless to weary my reader with details, suffice it to say that I was able to satisfy the High Court that the case was not one for confirmation.

They reversed the sentence and acquitted the ill-starred ekka driver.

His plucky little wife nearly went mad with joy, and wanted to renew the boot-embracing business, but my bearer rescued me and sent her off to Saharanpur by the evening mail.

"Why warn't there an aleybi, Sam?"

Like the immortal Sam Weller's father, the first idea of a native in trouble is to prove an alibi, which is rather a bad plea if the real one should happen to be self-defence!

There had been a grand fight out at

Binrabun, a place of great sanctity near Muttra, between two rival Brahmin families, and two men had been killed.

Both parties were run in, and I was sent for to defend one of them.

Now as the other side had trespassed on our land, and also struck the first blow, I did not feel much anxiety.

But imagine my feelings when my clients, fifteen in number, all pleaded alibis.

The Magistrate, a very jolly fellow, burst out laughing, and wanted to know where my self-defence came in?

To prove the alibis they had eighty-four witnesses.

Heroic measures were imperative, and the case was adjourned for an hour to give me time to knock sense into my clients, at the end of which time I was able to inform the Court that they withdrew their pleas and would tell the truth.

With much trembling the first accused began —

"Truly, your Honour, I was there, but directly the fighting began I ran away."

Again the Magistrate's fat sides shook with laughter, and my poor self-defence looked silly.

However, the other fourteen had profited by my hour's lecture on the advantages of speaking the truth, and boldly told what had happened, which, agreeing as it did with the police investigations held on the spot, was enough to send my men rejoicing, and doubtful as to the all-curative power of an alibi.

> "He wrecks his health and wealth on courtesans,
> And rolls himself in carrion like a dog."
>
> *Queen Mary.*

GUTARU MUL, URF DWARKA DASS.

Something like a client this! Mounted on a fiery chestnut, escorted by half-a-dozen syces and chuprassis, he looks promising as a fee producer. He turns out to be a young merchant whose extravagant ways are the scandal of the Agra bazaar, and who is fast squandering his capital on black-eyed houris and fast-trotting walers.

He may as well speak for himself, which he is quite able and willing to do!

"Your Honour doubtless knows Hashim Ali, the city Kotwal? Yes! Well, I need scarcely add that he is a bad man and my bitterest enemy! He has trumped up a perfectly false case against me, and intends disgracing me for ever. He has many witnesses, for all men fear him, and will swear whatever he bids them." (I had heard similar accusations so often that this little prelude did not much affect me.) "Now, Sahib, he had me arrested yesterday for having three nights ago entered the house of the celebrated dancing-girl Alabundi, against her wish, and beaten her servants, abusing her foully all the time. He pretends the delay in executing the warrant was due to my keeping out of the way, which is false. Alabundi, alas, hates me because the charms of a younger woman caused me to cease visiting her, and she will swear to whatever the Kotwal chooses. Is she not his mistress?" (Evidently a very immoral young man. He will have to pay a swinging big fee for taking me into such low company!) "Luckily I can prove an alibi. No, no, Sahib, not a common alibi with two anna witnesses. A real, honest alibi supported by documentary evidence. Look here, Sahib, the pretended assault took place on the 12th inst.; now here is an invitation from a friend in Hattras, dated the 10th, inviting me to a wedding. And here on the 12th is a letter written by me from Hattras to my uncle in Agra. And here, dated the 13th, is another letter written by me to my friend, telling him of my safe return."

Each letter was in an envelope; each envelope bore the postal marks duly dated. Hattrass is, or rather was then, a ten hours' railway journey from Agra. It looked an uncommonly pretty answer to the charge, and I undertook the defence with a clean heart. Every bazaar loafer and Budmash in the good town of Agra came to hear the case. How that Court stank! Whew!

Considering, as I did, that the case was a trumped up affair, I cross-examined at length, but to my great disgust got little good thereby, but our defence was unanswerable. Postal authorities examined the envelopes and declared the stamped dates to be genuine.

Amid wild excitement Gutaru Urf (*alias* Dwarka Dass) was acquitted. Kindly note the little *alias*. My client used both names. His friend in Hattras was similarly endowed, being known as Dwarka Dass, *alias* Gutaru. Do you see how it was done?

The Hattras friend had daily correspondence with the firm of which my client was the nominal head, and it was easy to hunt up two envelopes addressed to Hattras and one to Agra. This done, three letters were written and slipped into the duly stamped and genuine covers. The double name saved the necessity of tampering in any way with the precious envelopes. How simple! But neither the prosecution, nor the really clever Magistrate who tried the case, nor your humble servant guessed how it was done. The scamp Gutaru explained it to me some years later.

"MEN WERE DECEIVERS EVER."

Mrs. O'Flaherty honoured me with a morning call. I say honoured advisedly, because her visits were like those of the angels, she being far too busy, as a rule, in aiding and abetting ladies about to add to the next census returns.

"Shure, sorr, I've come to see you on a bit of business, but whisper now, are ye shure that none of those black-skinned divils of servants are lishening?"

Mrs. O'Flaherty satisfied her mind fully on this point, and resumed her seat near me.

"Is it true, sorr, that a man can be punished in this country for committing—saving your presence, sorr—adultery?"

I explained to her that under certain circumstances he could,

"Very well, sorr; then I want Mr. O'Flaherty to be punished."

The breath left my body to think that O'Flaherty, a man married since fifteen years, with five children, should have been making such a fool of himself.

"Did you catch him in *flagrante delicto?*" said I.

"Yes, sorr," says she; "leastways I caught him in the back kitchen making sheep's eyes at Janki, our sweeper's wife."

"But my dear madam, is that all you have to complain of against your husband?"

"And, Holy Virgin, isn't that enough? Shure, if adultery is punishable, conduct leading to it must be punishable too?"

I sympathized with and sleuthered down the good lady, and tried to persuade her that there was not much amiss, but her last words as she went away were—

"Ah, you men, you're all just play-boys and desavers."

CHAPTER IV.

"CARPET-BAGGING" is the opprobrious epithet by which we generally speak of the out-station work to which juniors must look for much of their professional income. Never mind; what's in a name? Even though baths, sleep, and work do get rather mixed up upon some of these forays, that heavy rupee bag will help to console you.

Should these lines ever meet the eye of an ambitious youth going out to India to make his fortune as a barrister, let him thankfully accept the following tip. In all his little travels carry a small but judiciously packed hamper of eatables, a tin of soup, some potted meats, and a bottle of whisky. He hereby minimizes the chances of death from starvation and from cholera. If his servant is worth his salt he will examine all the cooking vessels, and thereby save his Sahib the hideous pains which result from badly tinned pots and pans. *Crede experto!*

Does my old friend H—d remember that scorching day at Futehgarh, when he found me, poor griff that I was, in high fever, without ice, and shrinking from a nauseous-looking curry, sole object of the Dak Khansamah's culinary art! That worthy Samaritan promptly produced iced pegs, a cold saddle of mutton, pickles and other delicacies, and before his dainty fare and genial welcome the fever fled, and I was a man again. As a charming young German lady once said, "In India you must flake yourself," a rather literal translation of *Sie mussen sich pflegen!*"

Few men choose the rainy season for travelling, rivers being unpleasantly high, and fever a somewhat too plentiful commodity, but if one has the luck to start after a deluge and get back before the next the journey is delightful.

Everything is reviving after the long burning summer, greens of every shade take the place of the brown tints which have so long prevailed, the village cattle no longer stir one to pity by their starving, moribund appearance; on the contrary, a vague distrust fills the mind as to their impending death from apoplexy. How that ugly old buffalo is enjoying his mud bath yonder, whilst a crow perched on his broad back is making a square meal on the nameless myriads there resident.

The village tank resumes its importance as the favourite and fashionable rendezvous; in its pellucid depths men bathe and brush their teeth, women wash bright coloured linen and brown coloured babies, screaming and laughing all the time; brass lotahs and cooking pots are here scoured till they shine like gold; two ponies are being washed and emerge looking "dimnition moist;" cholera germs, typhoid fever, and such other little trifles may also be at work round the village tank, but what cares the mild Hindu? His fathers lived thus, why should not he?

Yea, verily, my civilized Aryan brother, you who have spent three years in London and been made much of by the Bayswater maidens, though you sport faultless garments at the Collector Sahib's at home, and believe in Gladstone and other devils, yet will you return to habits and customs, to which the village tank is by comparison sweet and clean.

Great Scott, where am I drivelling to? I wanted to say something about a lovely drive from Bareilly to Pilibeet, and instead have fallen foul of a tank; softening of the brain evidently.

A break in the rains and five days since the last shower means (oh, sapient T. G., who found the climate of India so pleasant) that it was hot as hell, and that even at ten p.m. breath came short and hard, lying down misery, and sitting up an impossibility!

The inside of a dak ghari looked too like a hearse, so I considerately put my bearer and traps there, and had some bedding spread on the roof, a rope round my waist in case of any walking in my sleep, and off we go. For over an hour we gallop on through silence and darkness, but as pitying our loneliness a moon, not a round fat ugly moon, but a dainty silver crescent, crept upwards, the stars took courage and turned up their wicks to fullest blaze, and some of the younger and more frivolous ones played a game of post, leaving golden footsteps to mark their flight. The dark old jungle must have become jealous at the heavens having such bonnie times, and called loudly to all the sprites and fairies sheltered in its depths to awake and show their powers. They came, and soon from branch to branch darted fire-flies ablaze with light, whilst the earth far and near was sprinkled with diamonds and rubies, called by the foolish glow-worms! Heathen that I was to fall asleep amid such joyous company, and well punished by the unpleasant awakening outside the dâk bungalow, where the sight of a leggy "murghi" having its neck twisted, told me what my breakfast would consist of.

REBUS IN ARDUIS.

Travelling during the rains is not unalloyed bliss, as I found to my cost in a journey which I made against time from Allahabad to a place in the central provinces called Pachmari, erroneously supposed by the Government of India to be a sanatorium.

And the way I came to undertake it was this:—

In a consultation held on a certain Friday morning with my senior about a case of considerable importance, we came to the conclusion that a document was absolutely necessary, and must be produced on the Monday following before eleven a.m.

After telegraphing ahead to have a dâk laid, I took the evening mail down country, which landed me at 10.30 the next morning at the little station of Peparia, whence a good road leads right away up to Pachmari.

I was soon galloping behind a pair of ponies towards the foot of the hills.

"How does the Sahib intend to cross the river?" demanded the Tonga driver.

"Why, on the horse ferry, of course," I replied.

The man smiled and said no more, but when we soon after reached the river I could see for myself that no power on earth could get the big horse ferry across, and it was only by bribing some boatmen heavily that I got myself taken over in a small boat.

Whew! how the tree trunks swirled and raged round our cranky craft, and how pluckily the poor fellows faced the danger.

Once safe across, I had to walk four miles

before there was any hope of getting a pony, so I pushed on ahead without losing any time; at length at Singanama I procured a mount, an evil-looking brute, all bones and white of eye, who, so far from appreciating my friendly advances, rose on his hind legs and knocked me over with a well-directed blow from his near forehoof, which of course did not tend to improve my temper, and I rib-roasted him pretty severely when we got under way.

But this scandalous neglect of Dr. Watts' teaching soon brought its own punishment, for as I was walking my gallant steed up a part of the road with a sheer drop on the near side of, I should be afraid to say how many hundred feet, the brute suddenly jibbed so close to the edge that my left stirrup was dangling over the precipice.

In vain I petted him, and addressed him in the most endearing terms known to me in Hindustani and English; in vain I tried to outlive his patience by sitting still; not an inch would he move from his dangerous position. At length, in a perfect fit of frenzy, I jumped off his back on the off side, and tried to shove him over into the depths below, but alas! the mild Hindu was again too much for the white faced, and quick as lightning he nipped out of the way with a most unpleasant flourish of iron heels, and left me to climb the last few miles into Pachmari on foot.

It was past ten o'clock the next morning before the document wanted was available, and so there was no time to lose on the home journey.

When I got to the river, to my disgust no boatmen could be got for love or money to venture across, and it was only after a bribe of twenty rupees that ten of them undertook to swim across, carrying me on their heads.

They lashed an old chair to a couple of bamboos, and seating me on it, took to the water in close order. It was not pleasant, and we were washed about half-a-mile below the landing place aimed at; but "all's well that ends well," and I safely caught the mail train from Bombay, which ran into Allahabad early enough to let me have a bath and breakfast before going into Court at eleven o'clock.

Before the rains this river, which gave me so much trouble, is a miserable little stream hardly worth tucking up your trousers to cross, but six hours after the Monsoon bursts it becomes a dangerous torrent.

AZIMGARH.

Of the many places in the N.W.P. it has been my fortune to visit, the one I liked best was the lonely, out-of-the-way little town of Azimgarh. We can take the train to Jaunporo and thence dâk it on. The nearer to our destination the purer the air becomes, trees of respectable size take tho place of stunted bushes, and from the overhanging branches troops of monkeys chatter a cheery welcome. One of these, evidently the local wag, drops behind our ghari and throws Catherine wheels *en veritable gamin.*

A good friend, resident of this place, wants me to stay with him, but it won't do. The dâk bungalow is the right place for a barrister, where his clients can see him at all hours. Besides my friend has always got a new and strange wine for me to taste, whence result headache and weariness unutterable.

"Worthy Khuda Bux, once more let me taste your excellent mulligatawny, and the Seth will presently send round a dali of fresh vegetables; with these and some plantain fritters let a dinner fit for the Lard Sahib be served at eight o'clock.

The Seth is a dear old fellow, and as plucky as a bantam. How he braved the "Zaburdust collector Sahib," yea, appealed right away to the Government of India, is it not written in the memory of each dweller in the bazaar? And was not the "Ballishter

Sahib" his confidential adviser in that memorable conflict? Did not finally the angry official forget himself so far as to be rude in Court to the said Ballishter, for which he had to apologise openly, being, moreover, transferred to a meaner place? Oh, yes, the Seth and I have plenty to talk about.

Business over, come and visit the satin stores. Liberty knows them well. How do you like this piece of claret colour with the thin stripe of gold?

This yellow deserves more than one glance; a bit of colour this, worthy to be carried around like the celebrated æsthetic smelling bottle, but if you have a soul for green, what think you of these three shades? You may buy. I may not, as many yards will await my return, with the maker's compliments.

Now down to the bazaar to pick up some of the local pottery, black with silver tracery; brittle ware and cheap, but strangely effective. Let us rummage through this man's old brass store, perchance a find may ensue. A melon-shaped vessel with wondrous design and finish rewards us. Six annas delight the seller thereof, which three guineas may not purchase now. One more search, and a Ganges lotah is unearthed. How many fruitless prayers have been breathed down this narrow mouth? How many weary miles has the holy water been conveyed in this vessel? Swim on, ye well drawn fishes; dance, ye shapeless gods, around the lotah treasure trove. Henceforth shall ye decorate my humble home, and the sole pujah you shall hear, the languid voice of "Æsthetic Bill," with his "how quite too-too," or shrill-voiced Ammurrican girl's "Oh say, ain't that pufficklу bittiful?" I know not what she means. Azimgarh is as much Hindu as its neighbour Jounpore is Mahomedan; the state records will bear me out that the former has long been as orderly and well-to-do as the latter riotous and bankrupt. Whether this remark can be applied to other places must be decided by wiser heads than mine.

THE COLONEL SHIKARS THE DACOITS.

There are Dacoits and Dacoits; half-a-dozen starving wretches may in desperation rob a granary by night. Dacoity, my starving friends, and toko must be your portion, but the genuine article is a grim and unpleasant reality.

There had been a first-class dacoity in a village about twenty-five miles from Agra—a band of ruffians had rushed into the place, set fire to some houses, and looted right and left, but not being able to find where the local banker hid his wealth they seized the wretched man and tied his hand to a post, wrapped some rags round his fingers, poured oil on the rags and set fire to this ghastly torch. Having made a night of it the Dacoits retired into the Gwalior territory and thought themselves safe, as a few judicious bribes render Durbar officials strangely blind.

But they had reckoned without the Colonel, which was foolish of them. The Colonel was the D. S. P.—or in other words he bossed the police of the district—and Dacoits being under his most special care and protection he not unnaturally resented this sudden disappearance. Now, according to law and letter, the Colonel ought to have handed over the pursuit to the Gwalior officials, but having had some experience of how much good that would do, he did nothing of the kind.

It was drawing towards the end of May, and to say that it was warm would be leaving a fair-sized margin for truth. We had finished our usual rubber of whist when the Colonel said to me, "If you want some shikar come with me to-morrow." And in a few words he explained how he had through spies marked down the Dacoits into a village two miles over the Gwalior border, and how he was determined to capture them by a rapid forced march, so that no one should get away to warn the gang.

The Colonel had sent his police force of eighty foot and twenty mounted men out to a village about ten miles from the place he intended to rush, so we sent our horses to await us there, and after a late dinner jogged off in palanquins to the rendezvous.

At 4 a.m. the next morning the little force was on its way, but owing to the broken ravine country our progress was slow, and it was close on mid-day ere the blue waters of the Chumbul gladdened our eyes.

Horses and men rushed into the stream and drank and drank again. The Arab I was riding plunged his head under water till only the ears showed, then on again at a pace which forced more than one poor man on foot to fall exhausted.

We surprised the Dacoits, who had barely time to clap to the gates and direct a weak and aimless fire at us, whilst we drew a cordon round the place.

Finding escape impossible, the Dacoit leader, Gunga Din, tried to cut his way through, and might have done so had not his evil genius driven him to go for an old policeman who had smelt powder in the mutiny when fighting loyally for the Sirkar. Rifle in hand and a tulwar between his teeth he sprang forward and fired, then quick as lightning seized the tulwar and aimed a mighty blow at the old bobby, who parried it with a heavy old-fashioned pistol, of which he then pressed the trigger and sent a bullet through his opponent's heart.

His followers, thinking to escape in the confusion, fired the village and stampeded, but most of them were caught.

All of a sudden the Colonel and I heard soul-splitting shrieks from some burning houses. We dashed through a perfect wall of smoke and found ourselves in an inner court, where seven or eight women were screaming for bare life, too frightened to help themselves. The rape of the Sabine women was nothing to the scene that ensued; the Colonel grabbed hold of two damsels and charged out. I seized first one and then another and shot her through the flames. When all were in safety we had very little hair left, either as moustache or eyelashes, but to compensate we had a thirst like the Irish doctor's, who walked into mess one day and said, "Glory be to God, boys, I've got a thirst on me I would not take a £5 note for."

But, alas! what avails a thirst when there is nothing to drink? Our grub and drink, unable to keep up, had lost its way, and 6.30 p.m. first saw us breaking our fast.

This little campaign of the Colonel's led to a fine row between the Gwalior Durbar and the Government of the North West Provinces; acres of good foolscap were spoilt without coming to any satisfactory result, but dacoity received a severe check in the Agra district.

A JOURNEY LEADING INTO TEMPTATION.

A dozen or more of us were lingering over some decent claret, and conversation was growing slack when the rounded Milesian tones of the doctor suddenly galvanized us into activity.

"My dear sir, as a man of the world, allow me to tell you that if the right form of temptation be produced seven men out of every ten will yield to it!"

He might as well have flourished the tails of his coat and requested us to tread on them. Around the proposition advanced raged an Homeric warfare, and it was 4 a.m. ere the last shouts of seven out of ten ceased to disturb the club house.

Without admitting the correctness of his figures, it is, however, true that temptation, to be of any force, must take the right shape, and Jones, who would scorn a money bribe, squirms terribly if the hook be baited with beauty or social success, or heaven knows what his particular weakness may be.

That I did not yield to the particular temptation about to be related was doubtless due to the wrong colour of the fly, and not to my guiltless nature.

To say that I was hard up would but feebly represent the case. A bay Arab and a persistent bad luck at whist had between them taken my last rupee, and the sight of a very smart wealthy native banker, who promptly agreed to terms, was most acceptable.

Where he took me matters little, but the railway did not help us much in getting to our destination. Once there, strange to say the clients seemed in no hurry to present the necessary petitions to the Resident; on the contrary I was taken out pig-sticking and cheetah hunting, and allowed to amuse myself regardless of large daily fees duly paid. At one of these hunts I was introduced to the Resident, who kindly invited me to dinner, and followed this up by an invitation to play tennis.

It at length transpired that the elder brother of my client was kept prisoner in his own house on a charge of having embezzled 14 lacs (Rs. 1,400,000 !) of State money, and that the real object of my visit was to obtain his release. Three years had elapsed without bringing either trial or release, and proper action would have promptly secured him the former, but conscious, doubtless, of the badness of his defence, the worthy prisoner preferred to try other means, and after much circumlocution I was offered Rs. 25,000 to go and hand the Resident 4 lacs (Rs. 400,000), a proceeding which would, it seemed, open the prison door long enough to enable the worthy man to escape into British territory and rejoin his money bags, which had long been in safety.

"No, my wily Seth, not for me this honour, Taslim. Thanks for the sport for the nautches, for your splendid Christopher's dry Monopole, but no more, thank you!"

We parted good friends, and a week later both brothers walked into my house safe, sound, and free! M'yes! Are all men liars? If so, their account of how it was done is false.

"Early one morning, Sahib, news came that the Resident was in the X. Bagh outside the walls. I hurried thither in my buggy, salaamed and begged leave to lay a small offering at his Honour's feet on behalf of my brother. That was all, and the Sipahis not being on guard the next night we drove away and hurried hither." So lied the younger brother, whilst the elder man sat and smiled a deep inscrutable smile.

If true! alas for tho fair name that is of more value to England than countless sabres drawn in her defence. But, m'lud and gentlemen of the jury, I submit the case is not proved. . . .

Whilst on this delicate ground let me

hasten to say that nowhere in the world is greater purity and a keener sense of honour to be found than among the civilians and military men who rule India. The story just related forms the one exception to my experience.

When we consider the positions of trust held my mere lads we have every reason to feel proud that the breath of dishonour so rarely tarnishes the fair name of Englishmen. Of course false charges will now and then be trumped up, as in the case of Mr. Wilson, but, thank goodness, our Local Governments are rarely tuppenny faddists, playing to a native gallery, and such wicked calumnies soon bring due punishment on those who concoct them.

This last word reminds me of the brilliant remark a foreman of the jury made to a well-known Judge: "We find, me lord, that the case is a gross decoction!"

A TRIP TO SIMLA.

A friend of mine, about to be married, insisted on my going up to Simla with him to act as his best man; so in for a penny in for a pound being always my rule, I decided to take a good holiday and give myself six thoroughly jolly weeks.

My first care was to send off by train to Umballah two smart ponies to be marched up by easy stages to Simla, as a good safe mount is of great importance in the hills. My next was to provide warm clothing for the two servants who were to go with me. This, even from selfish motives, is imperative, as the natives get useless in the colder climate unless you wrap them up well.

A week later my pal and I were leaving Umballah far behind us, and the dâk ghari carried us swiftly through the night to Kalka, whence the long ascent to Simla, an ascent, however, which, owing to the splendidlyhorsed "tongas," it only takes a few hours to overcome. The "tonga" is a two-wheeled conveyance, to which the ponies are secured by a yoke loosely fitted into a sort of saddle firmly strapped on their backs. In other words, the animals are held just as bullocks in a plough, only that instead of the yoke resting on the necks it rests on the backs of its captives. There is thus much less strain on the shoulders going up hill and on the hind quarters down hill than in more conventional methods of harnessing.

We changed horses every four miles, but as I was racing my friend's tonga, and the drivers were as keen as mustard on the Rs. 5 "backsheesh" promised to the winner, the changes did not take long. When quite half-a-mile from the relay each driver in turn blew a blast on his horn that would have made Siegfried pale with envy, and by the time we galloped up our new steeds awaited us.

I nearly came to grief; as we were tearing along behind a fiery pair of chestnuts, they took fright at heaven knows what, and bolted; that would have only got them home sooner, but unfortunately some cattle got in our way, and in a moment they charged across the road and sprang up on the low wall which is the sole protection against a precipice deep enough to have made potted meat of us; their fore-legs were on and over! The driver gasped out "*Khench, Sahib,*" and khench I did. It was an awful minute. We pulled on the reins for dear life, and the stout buffalo hide held: first one horse and then the other struggled back into safety. Without more ado the driver, after making some very disparaging remarks as to their female relations, straightened the now quieted ponies, and away for bare life. He admitted afterwards that had he been driving anyone unable to help him the strain would have been too great, and we parted good friends, though defeated by the better behaved rival tonga.

Simla, at length. Ponies had arrived the day before in first rate condition, thanks to good syces and a warm kit.

The season had not much longer to run, but there was no lack of diversion, and balls, bachelor given, staff given, or stately vice-regal entertainments kept the dancers hard at work, whilst dinners at Peliti's and the Club brought calmer joys to the heavy-heeled brigade. London in the season is the only place, in my opinion, to compare with Simla, when Simla is a-going it.

Society here takes its tone in a great measure from the *pro tem.* ruler. Thus under the Lytton *régime* it was flippant and witty; in the Ripon days dull and cantankerous, whilst under Consul Dufferin it became eminently well behaved and fond of rational amusement.

An unpleasant peculiarity in these exalted regions is the frequency of nicknames, which are often strikingly suitable, as, for instance, the mother and daughter both pallid blondes, who were promptly christened, "the faded photograph" and "the unfinished sketch." And then there was the nervous, near-sighted young man, who always crept round a room instead of boldly facing the company, who became known as the "musk rat."

The fitness of this name will at once strike anyone acquainted with the movements of that objectionable little animal.

Then there was the tall, thin lady of an evangelical turn of mind, known as "angular Fanny, or six foot of virtue."

And again—but steady the buffs, the law in India as to defamation is so elastic that I had better be careful.

A well known and oft discussed feature of Simla society is the "grass widow." Poor little lady, of what crimes has she not been accused! She generally has a bow wow (Anglo-Indian for a *cavaliere servante*), who escorts and guards her wherever she goes, but *Honi soit qui mal y pense*, and until she takes to letting him pay her bills we can extend over her shortcomings the ægis of charity. Now for a few words that may offend, but which deal with a plague spot which ought to be removed; Indian society is, in the matter of morality, hopelessly inconsistent.

Whilst on the one hand ruthlessly ostracising anyone suspected of keeping a European mistress, it, on the other, allows wealthy old generals, haughty civil servants, or members of council to invite young, good-looking married women to keep house for them, her husband being always in the plains; the fair one receives his guests, decked out in purple and fine linen, and displaying more diamonds than usually fall to the lot of army doctors' wives, or even to the better halves of Cantonment magistrates. Disgusting hypocrisy!

It needed the energetic action of H.R.H. Commanding the Forces in Bombay, to open the eyes of society in that part of the world as to this mode of keeping a mistress, and if he returns as head boss he may perchance enlighten the Simla and Mussoori dullards.

Then, again, such is the purity of the moral air—apart, I mean from the presidency towns—that the *demi monde* droop and die, they do not exist; this is quite as it should be, is it not? And yet a quaint old story from the history of Venice comes before my mind. It runs thus: Disgusted by the unruly and licentious lives of the then *jeunesse dorée*, the Doge solemnly expelled from Venice each and every courtesan, from the richest to the poorest; three months later a deputation of respectable married men came before the moral Doge, and prayed him to recall the exiled fair ones, as the chastity of their wives and daughters was slipping fast away.

If you really are so savagely virtuous, why, oh, why do you smile so sweetly on those strange little three-cornered arrangements, of husband, wife, and the "*tertium quid,*" as I think Kipling calls the male attendant of the lady.

Why, oh, why always invite the three together, carefully placing the "it" next to her?

Society answers me scornfully that if the husband does not mind it is no one else's concern. Truly a charming state of things; if a man consents to his dishonour it is no concern of those who associate with him!

> "I care not for her, I,
> I claim her not, and therefore she is thine."

And to such an one I say with the Duke—

> "The more degenerate and base thou art."

About as unpleasant a thing as the mind of man can imagine is to ride four or five miles in dress clothes on a pouring wet night, and ride you must, or walk, for every rick-shaw and jhampan is needed to carry the ladies.

Get your tat into some covered place,

where you can tuck in and strap down your various wraps, and away with you; I lay you five to one that the rain finds a weak place in your armour before you have gone half-a-mile. *Kuch purwa nehin,* will she not be there, and who cares for dimnition moist and unpleasant garments, if the cockles of one's heart are being warmed? Perfect floors, good music, good supper, and the-only-girl-you-ever-loved-partner all combine to make Simla dances red-lettered reminiscences.

The Viceroy's staff, personally conducted by the evergreen Mil. Sec., are always ready for any bit of fun, and were it not that an A.D.C. has twice as many lives as a cat, Simla might enjoy a first class funeral once a week; to see them racing tandem round Annandale or tearing full gallop down hills is a sight for sore eyes.

The chief charm of this place is that every class of man finds his fellow; the reader, the musician, the Buddhist can find friends quite as easily as the sportsman or the carpet knight.

Men with work to do, from the Viceroy down to the smallest wheel in the mechanism of the Indian Government, find it easier to work in the clear bracing hill air than when poisoned in the stench of Calcutta, which fact alone ought to be sufficient answer to the miserable babu newspapers ever howling against the Simla exodus, and the expense it entails. But more important even than the health of our rulers is it that our children should be able to remain with their parents in a good climate, with education and amusement available, instead of either perishing in the plains or being sent away to England.

My friend's wedding went off most cheerfully, and sad to relate, instead of weeping on her mother's bosom, the bride was as lively as possible, and instead of looking ashamed of himself the bridegroom twiddled his moustache and looked very much the conquering hero, which bad conduct was punished ere long in two ways.

The newly-married couple had been lent a

house at Mashobra, about four miles beyond Simla, and were to ride out there after the breakfast. Accordingly at the right time round came two smart-looking ponies, wedding gifts of the bride's brother.

The lady mounted and all was well, when it suddenly occurred to some inspired idiot to produce a bowl of rice and throw it about; chickens might have seen the sense of being bombarded in such a way, but a well-bred pony failed to view matters in the same light and promptly bolted. To say the brand new husband looked a fool is putting the case mildly, and to repeat what he said, as he galloped off, would make these pages unfit for publication.

The runaway made for the church, and the steep hill brought him to his senses, so that punishment—no, it was not very severe; but now came the good man's turn.

The reunited pair rode on at a sober pace, and were within a short distance of their journey's end, when suddenly a few stones came rolling down and fell across the pathway; in an instant the pony my friend was on shied and backed clean over the "khud!"

Killed; yes, rather—broke his neck; horrible! What did the wife do? Oh, she bought another. What, another husband? No, another pony. Ah, I see, a slight misunderstanding—the pony was killed. My friend stuck to a rhododendron bush, and escaped with a few torn garments. Moral of the above being, Don't ride animals in the hills you know nothing about.

My pleasant holiday was at an end, and as fast as galloping tonga, dâk ghari, and rail could carry me I was making for Agra, where a case of some importance awaited me; but though important from a lawyer's point of view, its technicalities would vastly bore a layman, and a slight description of Akhbar's favourite town may be of more general interest.

* * * * *

"You air, I guess, admiring of the Tadge Miawl?"

"Yes, I was venturing to do so."

"Now, sir, I guess you've just read up in your guide-book that such is the right and proper thing to do—say now?"

I humbly submitted that I had never had a guide-book, but so palpable an absurdity was waived aside by this awful Ammurriccan T.G. who had unceremoniously accosted me as I stood gazing on my well-beloved Taj Mahal.

"Now, sir, will you cast your eye on those four columns, called in my guide-book minarets, and give me a candid opinion about them?"

I did so. I mildly suggested that from their simple unadorned beauty they seemed intended to bring forward and emphasize the splendour of the dome.

The offspring of the most enlightened civilization fairly snorted.

"Minarets, sir—not much. Four glorified factory chimneys—that's what I call them, and even as chimneys, sir, not up to much! Why, sir, in Ammurrica we have taller chimneys than that most nigh anywhere."

Poor old chappie, I could have wept on his bosom, to have come so many thousand miles and to have been so sadly humbugged.

Nay, gentle T.G., to admire the Taj is not given to everyone, but list, I pray thee, how the factory chimneys appealed to a poet —

THE TAJ.

"White, like a spectre, seen when night is old,
Yet stained with hues of many a tear and smart,
Cornelian, blood-stone, matched in callous art:
Aflame like passion, like dominion cold,
Bed of imperial consorts whom none part
For ever (domed with glory, heart to heart),
Still whispering to the ages, 'Love is bold,
And seeks the height, though rooted in the mould;'
Touched, when the dawn floats in an opal mist,
By fainter blush than opening roses own;
Calm in the evening's lucent amethyst.
Pearl-crowned when midnight airs aside have blown
The clouds that rising moonlight vainly kissed—
An aspiration fixed, a sigh made stone."

"PEEPUL CAVES," H. G. KEENE.

There is a subtle spell in the calm beauty of the Taj which acts slowly on the senses, so that many a one who goes quite prepared to be struck down from admiration comes back disappointed.

Many a time in August and September, when the Jumna is in full pride, have I cantered down to the Taj before sunrise to watch the glorious colours stealing swiftly over the land, then boldly plunge into the waters below, dark no longer, but faintly tinged with gold, and now with a struggle the rays have reached the white marble, and, deftly climbing, drape the cold sleeping building in various coloured robes, the first of palest pink, the next of yellow, but the last of brightest gold.

Having assisted at the toilette of my queen I wander awhile in the scent-laden gardens, chat with the oldest of the "Kadim" (guardians of the tomb), and so home.

But though the most beautiful sight in Agra, the Taj is not the only one. I doubt, indeed, if any other place is so rich, and how the globe trotter can reconcile it to his conscience to "do the place in three days" passes my comprehension.

Why, I have spent a whole week out at Futehpur Sikri, the deserted town of Akbar the Magnificent, and yet not exhausted all its treasures.

What earthly impression can be formed of such a place by wandering around it for two hours with a chattering magpie of a guide? It is merely a collection of red sandstone houses.

But drive away all noisy intruders and let your mind's eye reproduce the various scenes which have been here enacted, and the red sandstone will soon be replete with life and interest.

Of all horrors, to my mind the greatest is sight-seeing in company!

Moonlight renders this place beyond all description weird and beautiful; the sculptured heads of tiger and elephant cast fantastic shadows, and if the dainty daughter of Birbul and her attendant maids were to move across the courts, or Akbar's mighty self were to pace the moonlit marble, the watcher would scarce feel surprised.

This place was no sooner completed than deserted, as it was found impossible to procure a proper water supply, the Jumna being twenty-eight miles away; and it now remains a stately record of the skill and power of workmen under the Mogul dynasty.

Futehpur Sikri itself stands on a small hill rising abruptly from endless plains around, and the Agra sportsmen often make it their headquarters for some black buck shooting or pig sticking.

How well I remember the fight three of us had with a grand old boar in this neighbourhood; he broke cover and trotted away in a calm, deliberate manner, which said in language clear, "I have business in this direction; I am not driven there by all that silly noise you beaters were making. Ta, ta," but the pace with which we raced up to him, all keen on getting the first spear, soon convinced our fat friend of the necessity to move on. How fast a pig can travel would surprise anyone who has not tried to ride him down.

My companions were an Irish doctor, whose seat on a horse was as strong as his brogue, which is saying a good deal, and a hard riding gunner. After a sharp spin the pig began to jink, and first one of us and then another came within an ace of spearing him; but the gunner would not be denied, and with a yell that would have done credit to a red Indian, he waved his spear, on which the blood showed beyond doubt that so far the honours of the day were his.

All is vanity, even a first spear, if the next moment your horse will put his foot into a nasty, treacherous hole and send you flying out of the saddle on to your head, there to lie unconscious in unpleasantly close proximity to a savage old boar.

However, a guardian angel in the guise of the doctor intervened, and after a few more plucky charges we had the pleasure of hearing that peculiar grunt whereby a plucky pig alone confesses himself beaten.

Luckily for him our gunner had pitched on the hardest part of his body—his head, and but for the shaking he was none the worse.

But I am wandering far away from the sights of Agra.

On the way back from Futehpur Sikri, when still six miles from home, we can turn to the left and rest awhile at Sikundra, where under a stately edifice of red stone, surmounted by a fairy chamber of purest marble, with carvings fine as the lace work on a lady's handkerchief, the mighty Akbar sleeps, his Christian wife beside him.

Most worthy globe-trotter, believe me, a whole day spent in exploring the buildings and gardens will yet leave much to be seen, and yet you "do the place" in one hour.

Go home, gentle T.G., some day doubtless

we shall meet at a mutual friend's house, and then you will correct my mistaken notions about India; you will tell me of the glorious climate, of the down-trodden native, and I shall bow my head and weep to think of all that was hidden from me and revealed as by lightning flashes to thee.

Back again to Agra, and before leaving it, remember that, even if you scamp a bit your visit to the fort and to the lovely tomb of the Prince Etmad Dowlat, you must not fail to see the many skilled works peculiar to this favoured spot. Husbands beware, there is an embroidery in gold and silver which causeth the hearts of wives to desire greatly, but the price of which is great.

A LEGAL OPINION ON INDIAN SOCIETY (GRATIS).

You may have had considerable insight into the ways and constitution of society in England ere your lot was cast in certain stations of the N.W.P., but that will avail you little; you must go to school and acquire fresh notions. First and foremost, the easy-going manners generally considered allowable at home are considered as loud and objectionable, speaking in a whisper is a sign of good breeding, and a tall hat to go to church the height of piety.

Visiting becomes a sacred and solemn duty, for is it not written, "Twice a year shall every unmarried man don his go-to-meeting toggery, and call upon every Burra Mem Sahib in the station?" Yea, verily, and whilst he is about it he may as well do the Chota Mem Sahibs too, who are far more pleasant and amusing. It matters not that you can all meet at band-stand twice a week, and probably elsewhere the other four nights. No, sir, you must call, dressed in war paint. Wah, wah! curse me deep, the said calling!

Next, learn to be 'umble, however much tempted occasionally to say, "Go up, thou baldhead." When a senior is blathering worse nonsense than usual, be silent, look impressed, drink in the wisdom he pours out for your edification; thus will you be considered a nice young man, quite an addition, etc. But alas for the new arrival who ventures, however courteously, to question or argue; he speedily figures as "that objectionable young puppy," or under similar terms of endearment.

If then you have called on everybody and behaved 'umbly, you may be considered fairly started; but "go asy, or as asy as ye can." Are you fond of fast trotting gees? Luckless man, he confesses it; and in an evil minute you would have trotted past old Sneezum's mail phaeton. Young man, had you done so, you might as well pack up and go to Madras, or some such Eden! Trotting past Sneezum's turn-out has, socially speaking, ruined many a man; for is he not the chief man here, and are not his walers the fastest, most beautiful, noblest, soundest horses in existence? Be thankful, guileless one, that this has been spared you.

Now the next danger is terrible, and requires explanation. You may be as polite as you please to married women, nay, more, you may make love to them, unless, unless —what? Give you three guesses! Give it up. Unless the fair one already has a bow wow (*Ang.* admirer). You must then be most careful never to get in his way. In England we like such little failings to be concealed, but otherwise here, we proclaim on the housetops that Mrs. Graball's "bow wow" is Mr. Scratchly or Captain Jinks, as the case may be, and at all social functions they shall be placed side by side. (*Vide* precedence table.)

Furthermore, although you may be popular at the club and on the polo ground, I doubt your ever becoming a social success until you have fetched and carried at least once after the fashion of the bow wow. The danger of flirting with spinsters is self-evident, nor is it quite so easy to slip out of an engagement as at home.

In England there is a nasty radical notion prevalent that men must be taken on their individual merits, but here we look at matters differently. If a man is in the Civil Service he *must* be a gentleman; if in the army the odds are in his favour; if, however, he is in the railway he must be a cad. The police, as directly connected with the Civil Service, are not beyond the chance of salvation. Where barristers, merchants, and such like uncovenanted scum are to go, deponent sayeth not. These little distinctions can be so charmingly emphasized in the precedence arrangements of big dinner parties—a callow youth, not a year away from Wren's cram-cub seminary, sent in ahead of a merchant who for years past has been widely known and respected, or perchance a smart young sub, proudly convoying the last available petticoat, whilst a disconsolate ruck of black coats tail in behind.

Under such circumstances is it to be wondered at that merchants, barristers, railway engineers, with many others, who mostly have comfortable houses and can entertain in bachelor fashion, providing boiled mutton without capers, do sometimes combine and refuse all invitations from the Burra Sahibs, yea, even omit the biennial visit! Pariahs they become, but, strong in numbers and virtue, they care not. Imagine how perfectly correct and lively the stately dinners are after such secession. The finest antidote to Burra Sahib snobbery is the presence of a really smart cavalry regiment, one of the "don't dance, don't care a cuss for anyone" style; the charming innocence of the youngest sub who lights his cigarette under the very nose of his stately hostess, she who years ago interdicted the fragrant weed on her lawns, is only surpassed by the genial familiarity of the senior captain, who slaps the collector on the back to the tune of "Come and have a peg, old cock!" Sainted mother! "Old cock!"

There is a good old habit of calling a spade

by its name, which seems to be far more prevalent with cavalry men and gunners than with other branches of the service. Can it be that daily intercourse with the straightforward, hard-kicking horse tends to simplify and rectify their nature?

There are quicksands ahead that cannot be avoided by the most careful; they are only encountered after the preliminary dangers are past, when the "griff" has become known by sight to all men. The momentous question then arises, To which set or clique will he belong? Will he be one of Mrs. Forty-four's "dear boys?" or will he enlist under the flag of Mrs. Lighttop-Heavysides? This is a weighty matter, and needs discursive explanation.

The two ladies named above are and have long been the rival stars of our local theatre. The former, who is exactly 4ft. 1in. in height, with a *retroussé* nose, fancies herself in tragedy, and trains up all her admirers to demand all the most blood-curdling plays, whereas the latter, a blonde female giant, is, when not actually engaged in adding to the population, the devoted exponent of burlesque—skirt-dancing and the flip-flap included. Her followers are consequently frivolously inclined. But angels of love and charity, imagine how these two ladies hate each other! Their criticisms on each new play are fresh and vigorous! Once, however, they combined their powers of abuse to suppress a daring new woman who accepted a *rôle* offered to her. The combined attack was so fierce and successful that the new woman had brain fever.

Can you conceive a Galatea 4ft. 1in. in height, with a nose best seen by the gallery, or a giddy young thing in tights, a head and shoulders taller than anyone else on the stage, with a fighting weight of 12st. 4lb.? Can you further conceive these charmers, each with a band of devoted followers? Perchance the T.G. who said that what had most impressed him in India was the extraordinary fervour with which men made love to their grandmothers had some such scene in his mind's eye.

The ball-room is thickly strewn with dangers; guileless youths glide around on its well-polished surface, and only find out later how sadly they have damaged themselves or their reputation. The Indian Mrs. Grundy is a terrible old party, and does not stick at trifles.

If you would taste vitriol, forget to ask Mrs. Slimtoe for a dance! N.B.—She gave the last away three days ago; but, nevertheless, old chappie, just forget to ask for one. She won't forget! Ten years hence she will not have forgotten!

Mrs. Slimtoe is very proud of her figure, especially of the length of her waist, so long that it got me into trouble by an innocent inquiry "which was her waist and which her ankle," they being so close together I could not distinguish.

But worse even than not asking this

charmer for a dance is to dance with Miss Rattle before taking a turn with Mother Rattle!

A back view leads you to imagine that the last-named is a giddy young thing of eighteen, which impression is strengthened by her childish tones, but walk round and take a look! Thanks, one look enough?

Head up, young man, no squeamish nonsense here! You dance at once with that worthy old lady, or never dare to look at blooming Polly again. Ha! ha! he is dancing with Mother Rattle—bravo, young'un! Now she is asking him to guess her age (heaven send him sense to say 25)! Good! again she smiles! She will invite him to dinner—Polly will be there!—*per aspera ad astra*—and Polly is worth tho trouble.

Having guided my charge into safety I shall retire to that tent outside, where a little game of nap is going on, and where a certain little barrister with more brains than legs is sure to be found raking in the "oof."

Telemachus, the griff, has taken my warnings to heart, but he is a tender plant and bound to get married ere long, which being inevitable, let us introduce him to a model wife for India, and may he have the sense to find one like her. Come on, Telly, we'll go to Chota Haziri with the Topsawyers.

Though not yet 6 a.m. we find the "dear girl," as old friends term her, watching the ponies get their feed, whilst her pet terrier, Nipper, gravely awaits coming events in the shape of breakfast.

Tea and toast, eggs and fruit are served on the chibootra at the end of the lawn, and before Telemachus has finished gorging Captain Topsawyer puts in an appearance. Something like a man this. Over six foot in height, and the best bat, runner, stroke, and rider in these parts.

When as a penniless sub he married the "dear girl," endless prophecies of evil to come were indulged in by their friends, but somehow or other they kept afloat till the present billet brought them comfort and freedom from care. Who rides like the dear girl? Who can drive a tandem so neatly? Who dances or plays tennis so well? No one that I have met. She has many men friends, but even Mrs. Grundy never accuses her of flirting. It may be that her music, painting, and other accomplishments do not amount to much, but, harkee, Telemachus, this is the right sort of wife for you, not a mealy-mouthed girl who goes to pieces in the heat, and has to be sent home every other year.

Note also, fond youth, that the dear girl is well-bred; the others go to pieces morally under the unaccustomed attention they will receive out here. Fancy a girl, whose place ought to be behind a counter in William Whiteley's, brought out to an Indian station, where, with ten other females of the same sort, she shares the respectful admiration of seventy or eighty men! Of course her poor little head gets a kink in it.

To complete the lad's education in choosing a wife he must dine with our Chief Justice and learn to know and love the dear old lady, who for the last twelve years has at all times stood by and supported the old gentleman, whose health is far from good. No slight thing for a man returning home after a long day in Court to find a bright, cheery welcome, and to know that a small but assorted circle of friends will have been invited to dinner. Nor, indeed, is the fact that a careful housekeeper has ordered the *menu* altogether to be despised. Comforted, refreshed, and amused, the C. J. sleeps soundly and goes to Court next day with renewed vigour. Bless the good sweet wife! Long may her gentle influence be felt! Wherefore, Telly, my boy, if you do not fancy a wife of quite so go-ahead nature as the "dear girl," then choose a gentle, loving heart to beat for you alone.

Stay a moment—seeing nice wives will not suffice; a vision of earth's best gift, nice children, must be allowed. So come along, and we can avail ourselves of this invitation to see my three ideals engaged in the serious work of burying their old playmate Tweezer.

TWEEZER'S FUNERAL.

For downright grief and misery this funeral has never been equalled. Tweezer when alive was not beautiful, though had you hinted this to his three joint owners you would for ever have forfeited their friendship, which would have been a cruel loss, as three sweeter cherubs it were hard to find! The eldest is a brunette, the second is a fluffy ball of gold, whilst the youngest, a boy, must have dropped from heaven, as such purity of feature is not made down here. This wee lad rules the house, mother, sisters, and servants; consequently when poor Tweezer came to an untimely end, his lordship, after a frantic burst of grief, proclaimed his intention of burying the poor old dog with all honour, and everyone had to obey.

First, then, the gardener must dig a grave under the large nim tree, then a litter to be borne by the four Jhampanis should serve as the funeral car, whilst all the women folk were to wreath garlands innumerable. Invitations to attend the ceremony were sent to a chosen few. Thank goodness, there was one for me.

His lordship marshalled the procession in the following order :—

The "Mehta," leading Rags and Tatters, two favourite fox-terriers, who both objected furiously to the black crape tied round their tummicks.

2. His lordship with drawn sword !

3. The body, borne by four stalwart retainers.

4. The weeping sisters, limp and woe-begone.

5. The various ayahs and bearers needed by Indian children.

Thrice round the compound went the mourning band, finally halting by the open grave. The darlings were so terribly in earnest in their grief, whilst we grown-up brutes were consumed with a wild desire to shriek out loud. By holding half a silk handkerchief across my eyes and stuffing the rest into my mouth I was able to behave properly.

Now the earth is patted down, garlands are heaped high over the dear departed. Surely the ceremony is over? Not at all. To his sweet mother's horror his lordship says, "Let us pray," and down sink in deepest devotion the cherubs three. The prayer ran as follows :—

"Please, dear God, take poor old Tweezer up to heaven and keep him safe till we can come and fetch him; and, please, he don't care for chupattis," but at this stage the handkerchief was not enough, and I fled away.

Forgive me, my pretty ones, believe me

that my heart is full of real sympathy for your loss! Was not Tweezer, despite his doubtful breeding, very dear to me too; but, oh! the "chupattis" were hard to swallow. To console us all we must go for a ride, your mother on "Vanity;" Browneyes on "Caramel;" Goldenlocks on "Ben;" and his lordship on "Bella." Yoick forward, leave grief and care behind.

> "O Weine nicht du holdes kind.
>
> * * * *
>
> Du brauchst der Thränen viele noch
> Für deinen Lebenslauf."

Deeply stirred by the sight of married bliss, the rash youth has plunged into matrimony, but if he hopes thereby to escape me as Mentor he is very much mistaken.

To begin at the beginning, my sweet turtle doves, you have married on a strictly limited income, but for the sake of all your future happiness avoid getting into debt! This is by no means easy. The tradesmen will not send in their bills, and expenses increase rapidly; then comes a temporary tightness, and the good-natured native money-lender appears—the dear, easy-going old fellow, how obliging, how confiding he is. Wait awhile, till the 48 per cent. begins to fructify, and the decree is given against you; wait, I say, till you are no longer a free agent, but a blood-sucked fly in the spider's net. The life of a bachelor deeply indebted is far from gay, but that of a married man similarly situated is purgatory before the weekly bath.

A newly-married couple are not expected to entertain or join in many expenses freely heaped on elder offenders, consequently, if prudent, they can make a good financial start. In India we are always hard up, and there is not the slightest necessity to feel any shame in saying, "Very sorry—cannot afford it." Why, from Viceroy down to the last joined sub, are we not constantly bound to use some such formula? Look round at the various families you know struggling under a burden of debt. Does not the number terrify you? Does not the hopeless nature of their struggle make you resolve to face bread and water rather than fall into the money-lender's clutches?

Enough said about debt, but what follows is intended to be strictly private, as the subject is unsavoury.

Avoid, oh, my beloved Telemachus! avoid, as you would a cobra coiled up in your pet chair, the husband's friend, otherwise termed the *tertium quid*, or "the tame cat," or "the bow wow," or the *cavaliere servente*; kick him out, no matter what his name or form. Your wife needs no other protection than yours. Never mind if the third party comes in fatherly guise, chuck him out. Such grey hairs are not venerable. Byron's view of platonic affection is the safest.

There are plenty of men who will make love furiously to women whose husbands they do not know. Very wrong, no doubt, but these are not the contemptible home-thieves, who, under cover of friendship with the husband, steal away the wife's love and affection, to whom I here refer. Treachery! Yes, blackest treachery is the right name for such conduct, and if society would openly show its opinion thereof we should be soon rid of such vermin.

Old Bengal Joe—home these thirty years past—says I exaggcrate this danger, and that all friendly intercourse will be done away with if my advice were acted upon!

But no doubt I have become a grey-headed old recluse, unable to appreciate the beauties of social intercourse. Even as Horace warns us—

> "Nec dulces amores
> Sperne puer, neque tu choreas,
> Donec virenti canities abest
> Morosa."

But however dry and hoary, I can still enjoy the company of my compound pets and nuisances.

Strange though it may sound, I never

owned, nor desired to own, a dear gazelle, but with heart and soul I longed for a cow!—some such animal as the dear old uncle used to breed far away in grassy Erin—all eyes and horns. Pardon the description, for, alas, I know not the points of a cow. What of that? Can you not love music without playing the banjo? Well, then, I longed for a cow, and unburdened my heart to Raheem Bux.

"The provider of the poor can have many cows by giving his slave the needed rupees," was the prompt reply. True, oh, flippant Rahim, but the cow must be of a pure breed, giving endless milk. "Trust me, Sahib, my father owned many cows," and away he sped, freighted with a bag containing shekels.

Next morning, when wandering round the compound, I came across an animal which at first sight I took for a goat. Now goats play old Harry with the flowers, and so I howled for someone to drive it away.

"That is not a goat; it is a cow, your Honour, purchased yesterday." On such occasions what a comfort French is! There are some blood-curdling expressions in the French lingo which carry you on after English has run dry. I exhausted my French and my breath, but the cow remained. Rahim swore by the white hair in Mahomet's beard the cow only needed fattening. With a final "Fatten her and be d—d to you" I turned away. Does a cow generally cost more than three ponies to feed? Information desired. This cow (*vide* the Bunnia's bill) lived for six weeks on linseed cakes, barley, wheat, spices, and sundries unknown —six whole weeks and then died! The Vet said "Fatty degeneration of the heart, caused by over-feeding," but Raheem said "Kismet."

The cow being no more, it became necessary to fix my superabundant affections on some other animal, and luckily for my sore and bleeding heart the pony Hard Times came to the rescue. Not that she was exactly of an amiable disposition, as any stranger trying to caress her found to his cost, but, when gained, her friendship was worth having. A bright bay, with black points, standing 13.3, with long sloping shoulders and great strong quarters—weedy, no doubt, but game.

As a tandem leader Hard Times feared no rival, but it took me three years to find a wheeler able to trot up to her, and the pair travelled 14 miles an hour. Not bad for ponies?

When first tried in harness this little mare gave us some very fine exhibitions in climbing trees and sides of houses; she removed half the porch on one occasion, and crashed through half-a-mile of bazaar on another. Never mind, Machree, you became an angel afterwards, and behaved as such when we all went over that embankment together. One struggle, one movement of your shining shoes, and the "dear girl" would have been smarmed, as we used to say at Harrow; but "like a graven image" Hard Times lay till all was free, then sprang up unhurt.

There are moments we do not care to recall; of these I reckon the sudden death of Hard Times, some years later, as one.

> "For the good steed, his labours o'er,
> Stretched his stiff limbs to rise no more."

Wherever good horses go after death, there is the bonnie bay.

Under the head of nuisances, Miss Judy, the wee monkey, deserves a foremost place; she is no respecter of persons, and pulls the white moustache of the General with utmost composure. The amount of mischief that imp gets through in the day is incredible; she upsets the servants' cooking pots, steals the mali's chupatti, pulls the khit's puggari off, jumps on the syce's brown baby left in the blazing sun by its fond parents; then, tired of outdoor sports, Judy comes into my office, an ink bottle catches her eye, she pours the contents on the floor, to escape condign punishment she flees gibbering and swearing in a most unlady-like manner up the punkah frame, and waits till the clouds roll by. But with all her naughty tricks the monkey girl is very affectionate, and dearly loves being carried about like a baby; to show her approval she will then gently stroke my eyebrows with soft velvety little fingers. Jealous too is the wee one, and bit me hard for daring to stroke Nipper whilst she was to hand. Is she really only one year old? Those wrinkles might have been there a hundred years or more, but the transmigration of souls explains this. Judy, in her former state, was a wicked Hindu Princess, who failed to perform suttee over her husband's body, hence her punishment.

This explains, too, why any attempt to dress her in ordinary stuffs ends in rags and failure, whereas a small silken robe is worn proudly; a woman's heart with its myriad subtleties beats 'neath the little monkey frame.

Next in wickedness comes the "minah!" Oh, the noise and the language! "Soor ka butcha," "ulla," "you d—d good-for-nothing scamp;" cat-calls and whistles poured from that bird all day, a proof that the Tommy who sold it had not lied when he said "the bird talked for all the world like a Christian!" Query the Christianity?

All this I bore, till the bird learnt the vowel-call, then we parted. The vowel-call goes thus: a man named, let us say "Raimana," is two miles off, and you desire to draw his attention, yell out, "Oh, Raimana," then "Oh, Raimane," then "Oh, Raimano, Raimani, Raimanu," da capo if necessary, and ever crescendo.

The bird learnt this in May, a bad month for the temper, so I opened his cage and bade the captive go free. In the following September I awoke to the tune of "Oh, Raimana!" The minah had returned!

Now ought Tom to be classed under the head of nuisances? No, dear old dog, you were a nuisance, but you are a pet, you rough and rugged specimen!

Though born in India, Tom's parents were English, and he himself a thorough John Bull in his sublime inability to believe himself beaten; seven pariah dogs tackled him one day, and though tattered and torn the white dog gave them all snuff.

When his first master went to the front he gave me Tom, but for many months the dog refused to ratify the transfer, and treated me with chilling indifference; one day, however, a bad touch of fever kept me prisoner. Tom marched into the room, took a critical sniff around, laid down beside me and refused to leave. From that hour we were inseparable.

How he hated cats! He treed a poor cat at seven-thirty one blazing morning in June and was found at eleven o'clock still watching his victim; we dragged him away, but the wretched cat had to be lifted down, its tongue was black and swollen from that merciless heat. Tom says I am no sportsman, but I don't care; cats are lovely creatures, and dogs are brutes to worry them.

If Tom disliked cats, Nellie, the handsome fox terrier, hated ladies! Believe me, when my chum and I were expecting angel visits Nellie had to be tied up. Ask that charming Mrs. Vaile, who, proud of having kept a tiger two years as a pet, scorned to be routed by a small dog. What was her fate? Did she not retreat ignominiously?

Then, again, although we had many dogs, Nellie allowed none of them inside the drawing-room. An armchair was reserved for her, and woe to the luckless stranger who sat therein. Sweet Nell, you were a vixen even before you were a terrier.

The belle of the place was Dinah, my chum's liver and white spaniel; her eyes were stars of morning, her silky coat the admiration of all. As became her sex, she allowed strangers to pay her respectful homage so long as her lord and master kept near her, but if his long legs vanished round the corner, Dinah, with a short apology, left in pursuit. The *entente cordiale* between these two was perfect!

Dinah had a first-class seat in a buggy, and was tremendously fond of driving, but it was amusing how cute she got about which horses were safe and which troublesome. For a whole fortnight that her master was breaking in a new purchase Dinah declined to go with him, and for the time patronized my steadier conveyance.

No professional beauty could behave better when being photographed; with one skilful shake she would display the long silky ears to greatest advantage, present the pretty side of her face, and remain motionless till the cap resumed its position.

Beauty has its drawbacks, as her ladyship found every morning after our early scamper, when the mehta caught her, sadly reluctant, to go and be washed; the bath with its subsequent rubbing, brushing, and combing occupied a whole hour.

My chum was generally considered to be somewhat of a misogamist, most foolish idea, as in truth he was far too much of a gentleman to be anything of the kind, but he certainly was not complimentary to the sex when, in answer to a lady who was chaffing him about not getting married, he rapped out, "Well, I'll marry when I can find anyone as pretty and honest as Dinah!" The brute!

Having strolled round the Compound, you may prefer to go home; if, however, the mysterious realm of Bohemia has any charm for you, be persuaded to stay and make the acquaintance of two men who trouble society but little. That gentle cat, Mrs. Nivlock, always speaks of the first of them as "that old reprobate!" and of the other as "that black man!" Never mind, abuse from this quarter is a sure certificate that the victim is worth knowing, and so come along to where my friends await you under the title.

GOATS AND THEIR GHOSTS.

If you had gone to church last Sunday instead of loafing around the Compound in that disreputable old smoking suit, you would at once grasp who are meant by the term "goats." The Padre Sahib made it quite clear that the sheep are persons on the Government House visiting list who go to church, the goats being reprobates who neither bow to the Lieutenant-Governor nor do puja in orthodox fashion.

Despite the thunders of the church, let us now go and make the acquaintance of two goats; with a little pressure they will tell us many things which, to put it mildly, will surprise us.

Talk of the devil, here comes one of the Bohemians we were about to visit, a high dog-cart with red wheels, a tandem of undeniable walers, syces in brown and gold, and a big, jolly-looking driver. The Colonel himself—who else speaks in tones of thunder?—wants me to go back with him for three days' pig-sticking! My gees can start at once; servants must find an ekka.

Temptation of the right kind this; I yield. We shall have tiffen here, smoke awhile, rest awhile, and then the walers must show what time they make over ten miles of pucka road.

Meantime, it is more than level betting that with a little encouragement the Colonel will treat us to one of his unlimited lies, which he calls a ghost story.

By-the-bye, you don't believe in ghosts? Of course not. Might as well believe in Home Rule for Ireland, *àpropos* of which I heard a neat little story the other day. Some gentlemen were discussing how Ireland ought to be governed, and over the wine the old battle for and against coercion raged freely. At length the host, turning round to his butler, said—

"And how would you govern the old country, Murphy?"

To which came the unhesitating reply—

"I would, sorr, saving your presence, go down to hell and fetch up Oliver Cromwell."

Mercy on us! Murphy knew that to make a countryman of his love and respect you it is absolutely necessary to knock him down once.

But to our ghosts. What do you mean by the term, believing in ghosts? It never conveys much to my mind. A belief in ghosts does not form part of my religious convictions; but if you mean by not believing in ghosts that all men who say they have seen such and such visions are either wilful liars or self-deluded fools, then we cease to agree. Anyhow, the following story is none of mine, and the Colonel shall bear his own burden, and if any moral brickbats are thrown, kindly let them be aimed at his venerable head.

The Colonel is a strange old warrior who

has the extraordinary bad taste to prefer living on in semi-regal state at a Zemindari he purchased long ago to going back to the "Rag" or other haunt of the aged man of war. The old gentleman can still ride hard and shoot as straight as most young 'uns. May Allah shield him as he meets the fierce charge of his beloved pig, and may the holy mother Gunga save him whilst tickling up her biggest muggers.

The Colonel, I regret to say, is a rude old man, as may be guessed from his first words to me after tiffen. "Hullo, old penny-a-liner, do you want some copy for your next dreadful?" His grey hairs, plus a large and sinewy arm, protected the aged reprobate from deserved punishment.

A whisky peg and a Trichy being found to his liking, he settled himself in the best chair and spun the following yarn :—

"You have met Charlie Trueman over at my diggings? Well, he and I made up our minds to avoid the ghastly Christmas festivities of Gurrumpore by sneaking off for a ten days' shoot.

"We had often noticed a deserted bungalow about five miles off on the banks of the Ganges, with a convenient ferry-boat near it, whereby one could at once get across to some excellent cover.

"The bungalow now stands alone, but some thirty years ago there had been a military cantonment all around it, which had been abandoned when the progress of civilization, as represented by the railway, did away with the advantages of transport by river.

"A creaking, groaning bullock-cart, drawn by two skinny and dilapidated bullocks, and driven by a native whose full dress left more to the imagination than was desirable, conveyed thither the camp kit. Not perhaps enough in quantity or quality to supply the requirements of a T.G., as they are now made, but such as it was it had sufficed us during many a long day's sport together.

"We cantered over early on the first day

of the vacation, and though in anything but good training, managed to get through a fair day's shooting, returning to the bungalow in good spirits, quite prepared to do justice to the efforts of our cook 'Raheem Bux,' a man capable of cooking a first-class dinner in a shaving-pot over a penny dip. How it would puzzle some of our bumptious and self-confident English cooks to send up a menu of five courses from a kitchen range consisting of three bricks and a handful of charcoal.

"After dinner Charlie and I had a long 'buck'—*Anglice*, 'chat'—which consisted mainly of long deep growls at the weary monotony of bachelor life in Gurrumpore—of abuse at the bumptious arrogance of certain low-bred 'Burra-men Sahibs,' who ruled the social destinies of that enchanting station—of the hopeless depreciation of the ever-changing rupee, and such-like pleasant topics; which, alas, form too often the staple of after-dinner conversation amongst lonely bachelors in India.

"At last Charlie, knocking the ashes out of his fourth pipe, announced his intention of turning in, and went into the next room, where his somewhat musical breathing soon proved the soundness of his slumbers. Left alone, I bethought me of writing a good long home-letter to atone for many previous deficiencies, and was soon quill-driving at a great pace. An hour or so must have elapsed, and I was biting the end of my pen for further inspiration, gazing the while vacantly at the open door leading to the room in which my friend was sleeping, when, to my surprise, a tall, handsome officer, dressed in white uniform, with a large military cloak thrown loosely over his shoulders, walked into the room and came towards me. As he came within the circle of light thrown by the reading lamp, I saw to my horror that blood was trickling down the left side of his face from a hideous wound over the temple.

"By the expression 'to my horror' it

must not be supposed that I for one instant imagined the figure before me to be anything but flesh and blood, and the horror was due to seeing anyone so badly wounded. Springing up, I instinctively pushed a chair towards him, uncertain whether to do the good Samaritan first and ask questions afterwards, or to gratify my curiosity by finding out who my visitor was.

"At this moment a fearful scream from the next room made me turn round, and in rushed Charlie, with a look of terror on his face. He threw himself into the chair I had pushed forward, and, as I turned to apologise to my wounded visitor, lo and behold he had disappeared! After a few minutes and a good dose of Exshaw, my friend was able to tell me what had so alarmed him, which he did in these words:—

"'I turned in, as you know, old man, and was soon in the land of Nod. I dreamed that a tall, handsome Kashmirin was seated on a small carpet not far from my bed, combing out her long black hair and crooning some strange little song. Doubtless owing to the glamour of dreamland, she seemed to me to be lovely, and her shapely arms and ankles were well set off with massive old ornaments. Suddenly she bent forward, listening intently as if to approaching footsteps, and I was almost prepared to see a tall, elderly English officer come into the room and begin talking angrily to the native beauty. Up she sprang, and with a gesture of disdain turned away from him. In one instant he had seized her by the throat with both hands, and to my dying day I shall never forget the horrible sight as she sank down dead at his feet. I had been struggling to get to her and save her, and awoke screaming with fright and rage at not being able to do so. You know, old man, I am not much of a funk, but I will not go back into that room to-night, and you may as well sit up and be sociable.'

"Charlie's story, coupled with what I had

myself seen, made me quite willing to do as he suggested, so we woke up our 'Kidmātgarh' and made that long-suffering individual get us pegs and cheroots enough to last through the night.

"The next day we ignominiously beat a retreat to Gurrumpore, and were much chaffed in the station for the rapidity with which our sporting ardour had cooled down.

"However, as we never confessed the real cause of our return, we escaped the worst.

"Nearly a year afterwards our 'Bobbery Pack!'—shades of Assheton Smith, John Jorrocks, and all other worthy M.F.H.'s. How your souls would have rejoiced to have seen and hunted with this noble pack! Small in numbers — namely, six couple. Musical—m—yes—a little too musical sometimes—consisting of a couple of half-bred English greyhounds, a couple of native ditto, three animals variously described by their owners as retrievers, setters, or spaniels, two villainous-looking bull-terriers, and three long-legged, flat-sided, long-nosed curs, supposed to have been intended originally for fox-terriers. These incongruous elements, however, had given us a rattling spin after a jackal, and I found myself close to this same bungalow. Riding by me was a retired officer—whom debt and other causes retain in India, but who, despite his many troubles, is still a keen sportsman and a good fellow—and I noticed him take a long look at the house as we passed through the Compound.

"'Ah!' said he, 'many a time have I been in there as a youngster, when Colonel L—r lived there, but my last visit was 25 years ago, and I should not care to see the inside of the house again.'

"'Why not?' I asked.

"'Well, the truth is, poor Colonel L—r shot himself one morning after parade, and I was one of those sent for to come to him. Nothing could be done. He had held the weapon steadily to his left temple and blown his brains out. How was he dressed when we found him? Well in white—it was June—but, strange to say, he had kept his cloak round him on parade and complained of fever. The cloak lay beside him when we came in and found him dead.'

"'What made him commit suicide?' I ventured to ask, after a slight pause, due to an unpleasant sensation creeping down my back as I remembered my visitor in the bungalow.

"'Well, you will hardly believe it,' said my old friend, 'but he was desperately fond of a mistress he brought from Kashmir, and she died suddenly of cholera a few weeks before. This seems to have preyed on his mind. Il faut chercher la femme,' concluded the old misogynist.

"'Cholera, was it? Died suddenly, did she?'

"Ah, me! to think of these restless spirits doomed for years to undergo nightly those fierce passions of hatred and revenge, of murder and suicide. Need we the eloquence of the priest and parson to describe material punishment to us when the mind can suffer thus!"

I gazed sternly at the Colonel, but not a wink betrayed him. His *rôle* of raconteur was one he loved to play, upon the slightest provocation, with impressive earnestness. He solemnly called for another peg, and asked in sarcastic tones—

"Never heard of the Fakir's curse? No, of course not. A Fakir to your mind is nothing but a dirty-looking man. Well, my ignorant young friend, learn that there are Fakirs and Fakirs; some are dissolute scoundrels, others are good men and holy, according to their lights. The man I speak of dwelt in a small osier-built hut on the narrow strip of land below the fort. No dirt in his case, for thrice a day he bathed, so that between praying and bathing he had little time to do harm to anyone.

"Five years ago three youngsters quartered in the fort, in an evil moment, resolved to build a boat-house on the sand in question. This they did, regardless of the Fakir's remonstrances. He turned away to seek seclusion elsewhere, but not till he had cursed the intruders and warned them that ere the Ganges should again rise and fall they three should be no more, their accursed house be swept away, and he, the despised Fakir, should have returned to his beloved resting place.

"Smile incredulously, but take these three names and search for yourself. The first fell in a border skirmish, a Ghazi earned paradise over his body; the second broke his neck at that hideous water jump on the Dehra course; and the third was drowned not far from here.

"The rains following were heavy, and the river rose higher and higher; the strip of land was soon covered, and the hungry Gunga swept away the frail boat-house. Content with her easy victory the river goddess withdrew, and left the alluvial sand to welcome back the old Fakir, who soon rebuilt his humble hut and resumed his prayer and bathing."

It strikes me forcibly that the Colonel has been out so long in this heathen land that he is in a fair way to believe more than is good for his soul. If, however, you can make friends with one of those strange Fakirs, who live alone in jungles, you will be amazed at his knowledge and power. Living in daily contact with brute creation, he seems to gather wisdom from the serpent and strength from animals we dare not touch; the myriad herbs and plants yield up willingly to his hands secrets of healing which the proudest physicians might envy. Personally, I owe the recovery of eyesight to a Fakir. Something went wrong after a slight sunstroke, and everything appeared double to me. Eighteen months of misery, and the doctors decided to cut certain nerves. Two days before the operation my Fakir brought me a yellow-looking fluid, and bade me drop one drop into each eye.

"Diseases desperate grown, by desperate appliance are relieved, or not at all," says sweet William, and the drops went in.

The next moments were not joyful; fire, flames, fury, frenzy, and other f's seemed to be my portion. Then came relief and tears, apparently not idle tears, for when they ceased I saw straight again.

The Fakir smiled, refused any reward, and did not come near me for over a year. Bless him! Why cannot doctors do the same, fee included?

This digression is uncalled-for; let us return to our long-lost goat, not the Colonel, a still less respectable party this time.

In a vast orange-coloured palace miles away, beyond the furthest boundary of the civil lines, dwells a strange old couple.

No one knows them, or indeed sees them, save when on rare occasions, towards dusk, a barouche flashes past, drawn by glorious, wild-looking Maiwar mares, manes and tails floating far behind them.

Business about an indigo factory led to my becoming acquainted with Mr. Maturin, and when, after many interviews, he invited me out to dinner, I accepted with considerable alacrity.

Mine host was a man of about sixty, tall, powerfully-built, with eyes that blazed and burned somewhat alarmingly; his skin was dark enough to justify the contemptuous term half-caste, which in truth he was, though not as we use the word. His father was an English officer, who, in some border skirmish, was taken prisoner by the Afghans. A princess of the land saw him, loved him, and aided him to escape. Hence the mixed blood. Mrs. Maturin, a faded, limp-looking old lady, did not seem very interesting.

Old Maturin and I became very intimate; many a morning in the hot weather have I cantered over to Chota Haziri with him, to be regaled on strange and delicious food and fruit. From Bombay, from Nagpur, from Naini Tal, from the gardens beyond Simla, supplies came in endless profusion. Agents and friends, he explained, knew his little fancies.

Then, when mangoes ripened, we wandered about the glorious gardens, choosing here a "lungra," green and sweet, here a "Malwa," vast golden beauty, or a "Hurdwar," fit to make the finest Bombay mango sink through the earth in jealous despair. "Cholera for certain!" growls the doctor. Bosh, old Pills-and-Plaster! fresh fruit never hurt anyone.

One day a touch of fever was making life a burden to me—had, in fact, done so for the last three weeks—when Mr. Maturin was announced.

He looked me through and through, then called my bearer, and bade him bring out some kit for me. Without another word, he lifted me up like a two-year-old baby, carried me out to his carriage, and, before I quite realized his proceedings, found myself tearing along to the orange building. A huge, cool room received me.

A few minutes later an old, white-bearded Hakim stood by the bed, asked no questions, but made me drink a pale green fluid out of a crystal cup. I remember no more. Nigh on twenty hours' sleep held me, but when I awoke the fever was gone, nor did it trouble me again.

During my stay it was my good luck to hear the wonderful story of the great treasure discovered twenty-five years ago by Mr. Maturin.

Told in black and white it may sound false, but heard in the deep silence of an Indian night, on the very scenes described, it rang true.

TREASURE TROVE.

"Having been repeatedly told that a vast sum of money was hidden not far from my house, I spoke to our old Collector about it. He wrote to the Government, but the chances seemed too uncertain to the powers that be, who, however, granted me the right to any treasure trove upon payment of Rs. 1,000. The money was paid, now to find the hidden store. Three years were spent in fruitless digging, and I began to lose all hope; daily the Mahomedan priest of yonder mosque came to urge me on.

"'The treasure is here, O Sahib—treasure of mighty Akbar's time! My grandfather strove to reveal the secret on his deathbed, but, alas! the angel's flight was too rapid, and his breath dried away, even as the tree fades before the scorching wind of summer!'

"One evening this worthy and I were strolling about in the garden when suddenly, from beyond that great nim-tree, a figure appeared, beckoning to us. With a cry of 'Allah mehrban!' the priest sank to the ground.

"To suddenly see your sainted grandsire is doubtless trying, but the sight of some-one else's aged parent being in no way terrible, I boldly answered his invitation. He turned and led the way to the old ruined well beyond the furthest clump of bamboos. Here my guide again faced me—truly a glorious old man, with silver beard of prodigious length. Thrice he stretched out his arms to fullest span, then pointed due east, and disappeared. Sadly puzzled, I turned back to where the unworthy grandson had collapsed. He was on the mend, and listened eagerly to my tale. Now this ruined well had been explored stone by stone, and undermined in every direction, so, despite the vision, my hopes were very low. The next day we went to work ere dawn. Due east of the old well we drew a line, and measured out three such spans as a man may cover from the outstretched fingers of his left hand to those of his right.

"At the spot thus indicated I dug awhile, and soon struck against stone.

"A long slab of dark-coloured marble, six feet by four, lay revealed, firmly imbedded in a layer of granite. No ring or other means of raising this block was visible, but a closer scrutiny revealed a small red stain the size of a four anna piece, which when pressed with a chisel sank in with a discordant grinding noise, such as a blunt saw makes on hard-grained wood.

"Three distinct clinks and a whirl of wheels, then slowly the slab revolved, leaving exposed a small flight of stairs. Bats flew out, uttering indignant remonstrance, an evil-looking kerait glided past with ominous hiss, whilst worse than these a vast boa constrictor raised itself proudly, and threatened to enfold us in its murderous embrace. But in vain the guardians of the treasure strove to turn us back, the *auri sacra fames* possessed our souls. Pausing merely to obtain a lantern, we descended the steps and found ourselves in a small chamber, at the furthest end of which an iron door plainly intimated that the object of our search lay beyond its chill defence.

"Powers of darkness! What are those horrors? Two forms lean against the wall and grin a hideous welcome. One still wears a red puggari jauntily stuck on one side. His remaining dress betrays the grim secret of their presence! Luckless slaves these, who after toiling many nights to store their master's wealth, fell beneath his murderous tulwar, certain thus not to betray his cherished hoard.

"Oh, great Akbar, what would you have done to this noble assassin? Would a couple of dead slaves have seemed worthy of notice?

"Cease that long-lived grin, my luckless friend; to-night shall you rest with your less cheerful pal in a soft bed beneath the tall plantains, and a kindly Mali shall plant purple iris o'er the spot.

"The iron door, despite its formidable appearance, was soon opened, and we could at length gaze on the long-sought treasure.

"There, in a small square room, hewn out of the solid rock, lay bar over bar of shining silver, brick over brick of pure red gold, whilst three chests, heavily inlaid with steel filagree, disclosed the flash of diamonds, blended with the red light of the ruby, the blue of the sapphire, and the matchless green of the emerald.

"Success in every form is sweet, and I cannot deny that my first sensations were full of pride and joy, but these soon passed.

"After all I was not a poor man, suddenly presented with great wealth. Children had I none, nor, indeed, any directly dependent on me. The shining fruit soon turned to bitter dust in my taste. I could have cried aloud, 'This quest is not for thee.'

"We divided the treasure into three portions—one to the mosque and its endowment—one to the poor of the district, whilst the third I retained. Its value was £55,000!"

My most worthy host, who did not need this golden shower, why, oh! why could it not have been my fortune to follow up a long-bearded stranger and fall headlong over piles of gold and silver? The taste in my mouth would have been uncommonly pleasant, and high jinks all round have resulted.

But, stay, get thee behind me, Satan. Have I quite forgotten the teachings of my old friend Horace ?—

> "Frui paratis et valido mihi,
> Latoë, dones, et, precor, integra
> Cum mente ; nec turpem senectam
> Degere, nec cithara carentem."

KASHMIR.

The doctor kindly gave me my choice of the cemetery or of going home. I declined both offers with thanks, and, assisted by a very good and kind-hearted chum, made tracks for the "lovely vale" of Kashmir.

The railway took us as far as Rawul Pindi, whence by tonga up to Murree, and nowadays by tonga right away into the valley; but for an invalid such rapid travel was out of the question, so we purchased a jhampan, and hired eight stout men to carry me along by short stages, whilst my friend marched alongside, tender and careful.

We took twelve days over the march in, and though the scenery is nothing wonderful, the air improves every step you take, and after the plains of India comes to one as something joyous, filling the weak and languid lungs with new life.

Every ten or twelve miles along the road are well-built dâk bungalows, where first come first served is the only rule, but being old travellers we carried a small tent, and had nothing to fear from the rush of persons, all anxious to get into Srinagar.

I had an unpleasant experience on this march. A favourite bull-terrier always slept at the foot of my bed, and behaved in the most exemplary manner. Imagine my surprise upon awakening to find my blanket torn to pieces, and Nipper looking at me in a silly, dazed sort of fashion.

Alas, he had gone mad, and the poor old fellow now sleeps soundly in the Kohalla dâk bungalow compound. Poor old Nipper, all he needed was to be left alone, but if another dog did not leave him alone he generally regretted not having done so. He was a bad 'un to beat.

From the moment you first catch sight of the Jhelum below at Kohalla it haunts you night and day, a noisy, muddy, mountain torrent, till it gives you a pleasant surprise at Baramullah by suddenly appearing as a wide and navigable river.

The road, which will long remain a memorial to the skill of General de Bourbel, winds pleasantly along some 100ft. above the angry stream, now plunging into pleasant shade, now boldly cutting its way through solid rock.

At one place, just before Dumail, we found that some three or four hundred yards of the road had slipped away right down into the river bed, leaving a perfectly impassable slope, which could not be mended under a fortnight's hard work.

After some consultation with a friendly road engineer, we secured the help of twenty coolies, and their combined efforts got me round the uninviting passage. "Climbing up the golden stairs" will, I am certain, be a joke to that scramble.

The nose of my jhampan pointed heavenward, obliging me to stand on my head, an art most of us neglect after our sixth birthday.

My chum, meanwhile, found it hard work to keep his footing on Shanks's mare, and consigned Kashmir roads and landslips to the bottomless pit.

Somewhere along this march our gallant commander-in-chief, "Bobs," as the irreverent Tommy calls him, swept by us with his suite, about to visit Kashmir, and right well his lordship looked on his handsome little Arab.

He certainly is one of the neatest riders I have ever seen, and stands fatigue better than his youngest *aide-de-camp*.

May he live for ever, and may some of the youngsters he has trained be worthy of him.

Someone of our bigwigs always is visiting Kashmir, and has little idea of the terrible disturbance he causes in that miserable country. The villagers, no matter what the state of the harvest, are marched off in hundreds to carry the great man's camp and impediments.

Scores of cows are collected at the various camping grounds, stacks of firewood, oceans of fodder, seas of rice, and heaven knows what besides. Of course the bigwig and his followers take what they need, say one-twentieth of the amount provided, and pass on.

The remaining nineteen-twentieths fall a prey to the Tessildars and other official scoundrels.

One old man told me that he and his three sons had been ordered to wait at Dumail four weeks ago. They were now returning home, having been paid Rs. 7 instead of the Rs. 28 lawfully due to them.

Oppression, deceit, and cowardice meet one at every turn of the road. Would the Lawrences have allowed a native ruler to grind and ill-treat his subjects thus?

I trow not.

On again to Uri, which no one may pass without partaking of the good Spedding's hospitality.

Here, indeed, is a princely engineer, whose ideas on champagne are as unlimited as his kindness.

Two more marches up hill and down dale, causing endless "La Illah il Illah" from the Mahomedan Jhampanis, land us in sight of Baramullah, whence our life in boats is to begin.

We were fairly bombarded by boatmen, each anxious to put his boat and its belongings at our service; the word "belongings" must be read in an elastic sense, as it is often made to include certain smiling female relatives, whose easy manners have earned the fair Kashmirin an unenviable reputation.

The long legs of my friend, who was nothing if not virtuous, played freely among the obnoxious crowd, and we were left in peace to choose boats for ourselves and servants.

The boats are not unlike the Noah's ark of one's childhood, and glide easily through the water. The crew, four in number, receive the magnificent sum of Rs. 15 per month, which is all that a paternal Government allows them to claim. It can hardly, therefore, be wondered at that the "Mangi," as the boatman is called, is fond of backsheesh, and seeks by every means in his power to increase his miserable pittance.

A word *en passant* about the beautiful maiden of Kashmir. She is an unutterable fraud!

The Mangi women are coarse, common-looking fishwives, whose ordinary costume is a short, loosely-made shirt, and nothing else.

As for the other women one sees by hundreds on the banks of the river, all that can be said is that if their godliness is on a par with their cleanliness they must be a nice lot.

The worthy author of "Lalla Rookh" is, I fancy, responsible for many of the erroneous impressions which are prevalent about Kashmirin beauty.

No doubt from all we hear the wives and daughters of the Pundits are lovely, but they are strictly "purdah nashin;" if they resemble their young male relations they must be very fair, with exquisitely cut features, and very large eyes, with long eyelashes.

These Pundits may be considered the ruling class, and are, of course, Hindu, but the masses are Mahomedan, which makes the iron despotism of the Maharajah the more unintelligible.

Imagine starving villagers, Mussulmans all, to whom consequently the flesh of a cow would be most acceptable, being punished in the most shameful manner because a cow was there killed and eaten, the cow, forsooth, being sacred in the Hindu Maharajah's eyes!

The second day found us at Sopoor, well in sight of the Woolar lake. The surrounding hills were still robed in their winter mantles, and looked well-nigh as imposing as the Dent du Midi and its brethren which encircle the lake of Geneva; they wafted us a chilly greeting each evening, but the hot sun was daily forcing them to assume their summer clothing.

Several Shikarris gave us tantalizing accounts of bear in the neighbourhood, one fair sportswoman having just bagged five, whilst her husband had to content himself with three.

Living in boats is doubtless very pleasant, but it has its drawbacks. The morning bath, for instance, is apt to be a somewhat draughty performance, especially if a Mangi comes in search of a paddle whilst you are in *medias res!*

I found it for him and knocked him into the river with it.

Then the cook's boat has an unpleasant trick of getting to windward—

> "Betwixt the wind and his nobility!"

And the Mangis, unless kept well in hand, are apt to let their garlics and savoury stews perfume the neighbouring air.

But for a short time this lazy, even-keeled towing is very pleasant. When of an evening the long light skiff is brought round, cushions and wraps piled in with a lavish hand, and eight strong Mangis paddle you swiftly to your destination, you begin to think carriages must be an old-fashioned mistake.

There is some good mahsir fishing to be got near Sopoor, at a place where the Jhelum runs out of the Woolar lake, and some tremendous fish are taken every year, but the heavy rod and hot sun combined to make this sport impossible for me.

Whilst we were lazily working our way towards Srinagar we were daily passed by sportsmen eager to get up into the numerous nullahs, where black and red bear abound, and various forms of wild goat and snow leopard reward the more adventurous. By law and custom the entire shooting of a nullah belongs to the first who gets into it, but if he leaves it for a day he can be dispossessed.

To be in the height of fashion we had brought a small photographic kit with us, and after some frantic attempts, at length evolved some recognizable objects, but unless one takes it up in earnest and is prepared to spend a small fortune on it, *le jeu ne vaut pas la chandelle!*

All the bridges across the Jhelum are of wood, and extremely graceful. No doubt when Horatius kept the bridge so well of old the Tiber was spanned by some such edifice, but I have never seen anything quite like them in Europe.

We halted about a mile below Srinagar to see the procession of State barges sent down to welcome Sir Frederick and Lady Roberts.

The banks were crowded with the gaily dressed crowd, the deep reds and greens mostly affected by the women being a tremendous improvement on their every-day mud-coloured garments.

The State barges need upwards of a hundred men each to propel them, and then cannot be said to fly.

On one of these leviathans the newly-trained Kashmir band was indulging in a choice selection of popular airs; on the principle of counter irritation the music they evolved ought to cure all ills that flesh is heir to.

The Maharajah, the Resident, and Sir Frederick were penned together, each of them gorgeous after his particular fashion, and smiling away like waxworks at Madame Tussaud's.

Endless cannon boomed and banged from the fortress, bells clanged from all the temples, and amid a respectful buzz of admiration from the dense crowd the ruler of

Kashmir led his honoured guest to the Palace prepared for his reception.

Oh, Bobs Bahadur, jewel of my heart, why are you not at the head of a nice little force, consisting mostly of Highlanders and Goorkas? You could make everything so comfortable both for us poor Anglo-Indians, who need a better climate for our children, and for the poor Mahomedan population of Kashmir.

The first view of Srinagar, as one comes up the Jhelum, is decidedly fascinating, and the title of Venice of the East seems well deserved. It is only when approached from the land side that one realizes what a dirty hole it is.

As each new arrival comes in sight, slowly punted up stream, he is waylaid by scores of little boats, in which are seated jewellers, shawl merchants, fur sellers, papier maché makers, etc., all anxious to be allowed to inscribe a fresh victim's name, unlimited credit being the order of the day, and money a thing unheard of.

Beware, dear new arrival!

It is very easy to get into debt in Kashmir, but precious hard to leave the country without paying.

I could fill a good-sized volume with stories about the doings of some of the chief native bankers, but *verbum sap.*

It is now quite easy to get money through the post, and there is not the slightest necessity for banking any money during one's six months' stay.

Bachelors, when in Srinagar, must pitch their tents in the Chenar Bagh, whilst married people are relegated to the Munshi Bagh; at first sight the bachelors seem to have the best of it, but in May and June certain odours pervade the former grove, which leave little to be desired in the way of nastiness.

Driven onward by these odours we embarked again, and were paddled across the beautiful Dall lake, which lies inland behind Srinagar, to the Nuseem Bagh, a lovely camping ground, overhead gigantic plain trees and underfoot soft green turf.

Oh, Mangiji! here will we pitch our tents; here shall your skilful hands construct a Chattai hut, where Babu Lal, grimiest of cooks, may concoct his savoury messes. You and yours will, I know, occupy one of the boats, leaving the other for the two bearers and the khitmugar!

Now, then, a hammock must be slung from those great branches, and an awning fixed overhead. With books, fruit, and pleasant company let us rest awhile and fancy ourselves lotus eaters.

The unbroken stillness, the balmy air, the beauty of the scenery all combine to make one rest contentedly, which after the ceaseless activity of a business man's life in India is most soothing and restoring.

Nearly opposite our camping ground lay the Shalimar gardens, up which the lovely Lalla Rookh was wafted to meet her lord and master, Feramorz. Many a time do joyous parties paddle across to these shady groves, and the hearty laughter of ribald English subalterns disturbs the stately repose of bygone Mogul kings, when ever and anon they revisit this spot where so many of their happiest hours were passed.

These picnic parties invariably start out in the most decorous manner, in two or more large boats, but somehow or other the return journey by moonlight is always effected in small skiffs, *tête-à-tête*. The amount of sentimental bilge water expended thus annually is said to affect the rise and fall of the Ghelum.

Further to the right we can see the terraces of the Nishat Bagh, where the ruler of Kashmir takes a dreary delight in watching some cleverly contrived *jets d'eau*.

The Maharajah of Jamu and Kashmir is a miserable, decrepit-looking creature, whose personal habits and morality make even the Kashmiri Mangi blush, and would be far more in his place in a tread-mill than lording it over his miserable subjects.

His two younger brothers, Ram Singh and Amar Singh, hate each other like poison, and try to cut each other out in the most childish manner, as, for instance, Ram Singh had a tiny little steam tug built for him, whereupon Amar Singh promptly orders one twice as big. Ram Singh, I believe, is negotiating the purchase of a juvenile *Great Eastern*.

Since these lines were written, I am aware that the Maharajah has been decorated and restored to his place and power; but I care not, and the truth remains that to support so vile a despot and so contemptible a man is unworthy of England's greatness.

Having thus relieved my feelings, I may with a clear conscience turn to the real work of life in Kashmir, which is to frivol.

Barring, of course, the Resident and the worthy brothers Neve, we all came here with frivolous intent.

If you doubt me come round to the top of the Chenar Bagh, where some of the Royal

Irish have made themselves comfortable with their endless ponies and dogs. As we approach the music of a pig being killed rises clear upon the air; no, it is not a pig singing his own dirge, but thick-headed John and O'Leary are holding the unfortunate Tralee lad head downwards in a tub of water. John explains that this is punishment for having sown him up in bed last night.

The victim being released, our hosts promptly suggest whisky. It being, however, little after ten a.m. we waive the suggestion aside. O'Leary thereupon suggests a little "divarsion" in the form of vaulting the horse.

Most of us have done this in the gymnasium over a well-stuffed dead'un, but the same performance over a remarkably free kicking polo tat is, to say the least of it, exciting.

These gentle exercises are merely preliminary to whatever cricket or polo may be going.

Whatever the fun may be, trust the R.I.

to be in the thick of it. Their racing tats swept the board, and their polo team just walked round all other competitors, but if an Irishman cannot ride, who can?

There is any amount of racing in Kashmir, as the Punjaub sportsmen can march their crocks in at a very small cost, and once a week at the least there were also high jinks for ladies.

Talk of men being horsey, you should hear some of these fair ones after winning a race—grooms would be nowhere; and if perchance the lady can shoot a bit as well, her conversation will probably need explanation. A very favourite form of race was the "needle and thread" scamper.

Let us suppose five ladies compete; each is mounted and presented with a needle, which she sticks into her habit. At a given signal they race down to a place, where five gentlemen await them. Dismounting by her particular young man each lady presents her needle, which he must thread and replace, then with his help she must mount again and leg it home. First back carrying the needle and thread wins. How often ladies are pitched clean over the ponies' backs in these scrambling mounts, and how often pretty lips say naughty words at the clumsiness of the miserable men trying to thread a needle quickly, deponent sayeth not.

I saw one little lady contrive to win, but unable to stop her mad career she rode up a steep hill beyond, and owing to her imposing appearance when there was generally known then and after as "Miss Skyline."

Another amusement for ladies is the "egg and spoon" race, where each competitor carries a spoon, and tries to balance an egg on it. To do this at full gallop is not as easy as it sounds.

But, after all, boating is the amusement *par excellence* in Kashmir.

One evening, whilst paddling about on the lake, I saw a sight not easily forgotten. My boat was in the middle, half way between the

Nishat and the Nuseem Bagh, when the long rays of the setting sun crimsoned the waters from the shore up to my boat, whilst at the same moment the silver beams of a full moon stole swiftly from the opposite shore, and made a pathway of light up to where I lay; to my right blood red, to my left purest silver.

Ah, those moonlight nights on the Dall lake, gliding silently through the lotus lilies, and past the floating gardens, whilst high above the Takt i Suleiman stands out clear and guards the waters below from harm and evil.

As I was a cripple I was unable to explore the highlands of Kashmir, and so have no right to give any opinion as to scenery, but confining my remarks to the valley, I must say the Dall was the one and only beautiful part I could see, but then it was so perfect as to make up for all the rest. The Jhelum is navigable up to Islamabad, and thither we duly made our way, fishing, reading, and taking photographs as we wandered on.

Sometimes our camp would be in a lovely orchard, and if cholera and fruit eating have any connection we did our best to qualify for the entrance thereto.

To frighten away the birds the Kashmiris make long whips of weeds, which crack as loudly as a French postilion's, and are not the best accompaniments to morning slumber.

At Islamabad we duly purchased some of the rugs for which the place is famous, and providentially had a tin of Keating's best with us, which we applied freely before housing our new purchases.

One of the chief attractions of Kashmir to Anglo-Indians is the utter freedom from red tape and regulation; no levées to attend, no uniform to wear, dress clothes even to quite lately were regarded as curiosities—ladies going about in red skirts, very, very short, are often seen.

Most people wear "chuplis," things not unlike sandals, and so comfortable that boots become a burden for the rest of one's life.

Round the leg a cloth bandage known as a "putti" gives support and leaves the muscles free play. A very ancient pair of riding breeks and an old Norfolk jacket complete your kit, and leave small room for dandyism. Freedom of another kind is also prevalent, else, I pray you, how comes it to be tolerated that those two ladies arrived in the valley three months ahead of their husbands, each escorted by a *locum tenens*, who, strange to say, although bachelors, were allowed to pitch their tents cheek by jowl with their friends in the Munshi Bagh, sacred to married couples? Or how again, when some rain fell, did Mrs. W. contrive to let her "bow wow" share her log hut, as he was delicate? No one minds these little escapades; we all keep good friends, and enjoy freedom under all her shapes and guises.

Not many years ago freedom was so complete in this favoured vale, that ladies had to grow pretty thick skins before visiting it, *mais nous avons changés tout cela*, and the gaily-dressed boat loads of Kashmiri demi monde no longer shock the British matron's eye, at least not in open day.

Considering our unoccupied condition, and the perfect freedom around us, we are, on the whole, very well behaved, but the old saying about Satan and idle hands was forcibly illustrated by a wonderful duel which took place between a young Irish sawbones and a canny Scotch officer.

The gentlemen had a difference of opinion as to the respective merits of Scotch and Irish whisky, and when the military Sandy so far forgot himself as to say that "Irish whisky was smoked water with a flavour of the pigstye," blood alone could wipe out the insult!

The blood of all the Irish kings was aroused, and the doctor fairly thirsted for vengeance. Finding him relentless, we arranged a duel of the most bloody nature! Weapons, army revolvers! Distance, ten yards! Each shot to be by word of command. Toss for first shot! Kindly imagine the feelings of any poor devil waiting to be shot at under such circumstances!

The scene of slaughter was a long, low room, the walls and ceiling of which were of white plaster.

"Have you made your will, doctor?" asked one sympathizer. He had not. We at once made the legal member of the party prepare a will in approved form. Had he made his soul? I regret to say that the language with which he greeted this friendly suggestion looked very much as if he had not.

At last all was ready—the Scotchman grim and silent; the doctor, a bit wild-looking, but full of pluck.

The seconds prepared the weapons of death, placed the men, tossed for the first shot. "Erin go bragh," the doctor wins.

Are you ready? Fire! Bang! Missed, by Jove!

Now for the Scotchman. He fires, and

the doctor shudders convulsively as plaster and *débris* rain on him. The lookers-on gravely discuss his wonderful escape.

Five times does the doctor miss his man, and five times did he himself escape in a miraculous manner. Witness the state of his clothes.

The seconds declared honour satisfied, and we gave the doctor a seat and a glass of brandy, both of which he needed badly.

It was only on the following day we told him that his revolver was loaded with blank cartridge, whilst his opponent was given ball, so as to bring down the neighbouring plaster! Alas! poor doctor!

* * * * *

Srinagar was getting somewhat too aromatic, and it was yet too early to go to the hills, so we paddled down stream again to the Woolar Lake, exploring around it in a lazy sort of way.

One night we had pitched our tents on a

bit of ground some twenty feet above the lake, our boats being made fast under a sheltering ledge. Towards midnight a regular hurricane swept down suddenly from the hills and made a very creditable attempt to blow us bodily into the lake. The attempt was, however, thwarted by the gallant behaviour of my worthy chum, who, in fluttering pyjamas, faced the storm, and like another Ajax, defying the elements, held on to the slackened tent ropes, swearing all the while so lustily that the sleepy servants and Mangis at length came to the rescue.

I, worthless drone, lay snugly in bed convulsed with endless laughter. We finally took refuge in our boats, which lay safe and snug under the protecting bank.

This daring behaviour of my long-legged pal formed a worthy conclusion to his office of guardian angel, which he had fulfilled so nobly. Stern duty recalled him to the plains of India, and with a sinking heart I saw him off from Baramullah.

He stands six-foot-six in height, and the only conveyance he could find to his mind was a long-backed tat, barely thirteen-one!

He looked like a daddy-long-legs astride a caterpillar.

Pardon my ribald nonsense, dear old man, and wherever you go carry with you my most grateful thanks for all your kindness and care.

Our parting, however, as due to our English origin, was far from sentimental.

Doubtless on the eve of his departure I ought to have taken his hand and muttered —

> "Other friends have flown before;
> On the morrow he will leave me."

But I didn't.

Being now left to my own devices, I turned up stream, but the heat, the flies, and the loneliness soon made me contemplate suicide.

Honourable mention having been made of the flies, my duty, as truthful historian of

Kashmir, compels me to speak of the mosquitoes.

I had an idea that I knew something about mosquitoes before going to Kashmir. Once again I learnt the bitter lesson of how little one really knows about anything.

My introduction to a Kashmiri mosquito was in this wise: I was sleeping in my boat, when a loud noise awoke me. Firing a salute at the fort, thought I, and turned over; but, no, the fort guns would have burst if subject to such a strain. A Mangi beating his wife? No; too regular a sound. Then I became aware that some big bird or bat was practising flying near my head. In terror I howled for help, and soon had Mangis by the score hunting the deadly intruder. When caught they pegged it out on the floor. I asked the name of this strange bird?

"Mosquito, Sahib!" was the answer. It may have been so, but it looked more like a snipe, and had a fine contralto voice.

From further questioning I gathered that

this ghastly specimen was only a herald, and that others might be expected shortly. Plague of Egypt! Why didn't Moses try a few Kashmiri mosquitoes?

Terrified by this information, I fled away by night some miles below Srinagar, to the nearest spot whence the ascent to Gulmarg, a summer resort, can be made.

By a moonlight of utter brightness I started off in state, on through the shimmering rice fields, on past rows of silvery willows, on till the first low bushes told of approaching woods, on till the first pine tree greets us stately and unbending, and on when the deep, dark forest swallows us up, only to restore us to light and freedom in the charmed valley of Gulmarg.

The next thing to be done was to build a log hut!

Here is a recipe, which resulted in a most comfortable abode and cost Rs. 15!

(N.B.—*En passant*, the pines are most adjacent.)

1.—Make four holes in the ground, like children making mud pies.

2.—Stick four pine trees into the four holes; stamp them in with your bare feet (a splendid cure for corns).

3.—Stick two long and two short pine trees on the top of the upright pines.

4.—Nail long thin planks wherever you would prefer that rain did not come in, leave one hole for a door (the smaller the better), "lepe" all over with mud! Æsthetic furniture, piano, etc., are not absolutely *de rigueur!*

"Blow winds and crack your cheeks." I sit beside a roaring fire and care not. Yes, from heat and mosquitoes to log fires was but a night's journey.

IN THE LOG HUTS OF GULMARG.

Hospitality was the order of the day, from the sumptuous and generous table of the resident down to the rickety camp kit of the youngest subaltern.

One of these festive gatherings will remain engraven on my memory to my dying day, partly because of the stories then told, and partly because a ludicrous incident befell us guests on our way home.

The stories told I can reproduce very nearly in the words of the tellers. But as to their veracity I prefer to offer no opinion.

The first to spin a yarn was a T.G., but a globe trotter, quite *hors de ligne*, and a prime favourite; he was a retired Major, and what is more to the point, a bachelor.

Why the gallant officer had never married (despite advantages of wealth and good looks) was known to few, but our host's champagne acted as a spell, and we were privileged to hear

THE MAJOR'S STORY.

"I cannot remember a time in my life when I was not in love with my cousin, Lily

McAlbin; we had been brought up together, and had shared childhood's joys and sorrows. Time strengthened our affection, and when at last I had to join my regiment in India, our parting was indeed a painful one. Again and again I vowed to come home within three years to make her my bride.

"Her grief at parting, though deep and sincere, was quieter and more self-contained than mine.

"*L'homme propose, mais Dieu dispose.*

"Before a year was over Lily was laid to rest in the old churchyard of H.!

"The news of her death reached me just as I was starting for a trip in Kashmir, and in my deep grief I felt it best to get away from all mankind and bury myself in some remote shooting ground.

"Well, to cut a long story short, I was out one morning in the hills above the Woolar Lake, and had just fired both barrels at a large red bear when a cry from my Shikari warned me of the approach of a she bear, probably mate to the one I had dropped. The man had my second rifle, and if he had only rushed over and handed it to me all would have been well, but instead of that, he fired rapidly two shots, neither of which seemed to seriously inconvenience the animal. In a moment she was on him, embracing him in no tender clasp. I drew my long hunting knife and dashed in to the rescue. The poor man was crushed flat, and Mrs. Bruin turned her whole attention on me. I have felt the hug of a Cornish wrestler and the grip of a Punjaubi Paihlwan, but they were as child's play to the grip in which I now found myself. Luckily my right arm was free, and I buried my knife up to the hilt time after time in her ladyship's back and sides. To make matters worse we were on the very edge of a precipice, which, with but a few stunted trees growing on its side, sheered right away into a yawning chasm below. Firmly locked in the bear's arms I felt that we were beginning to slide down this horrible place; a few frightful blows on my back and head, a rapid rush through space and all was over.

"When I came to my senses, around me was black darkness. Groping around cautiously my hands encountered the dead body of the bear. I staggered to my feet and found, to my dismay, that I was in a living tomb. All egress seemed impossible; round me on every side cold, wet rock formed an impassable barrier.

"The horror of my position became too much for me, and with a long, shivering cry for help I fell senseless to the ground.

"How long I so lay I know not, but suddenly the darkness was illumined by a soft, pale light, and, clear as in the happy days gone by, I saw my Lily as sweet as ever. She pointed to the furthest corner of my dungeon, where, by the help of the light that now shone, I was able to see that a spring of water rose from the ground and escaped merrily down a passage in the rock.

"On hands and knees I staggered towards the pale figure of my loved one. She drew gently back to the passage made by the water. I crawled slowly and painfully after her, ever seeking to overtake the receding figure. The water struck icy-cold against my stiffened limbs, and the rock cut hard into hands and knees. But what cared I? At length, after a long and weary crawl, I emerged into the light of day, and saw my Lily fade fast away, leaving me naught but the memory of her smile, full of ineffable love and hope! She had led me from a certain and horrible death into safety.

"The memory of my angel love guarding me through those dreadful hours of peril has never left me, and so long as I can feel that she is by me, to watch with loving care my every movement, so long must I feel that to take any other woman to my heart and home would be to lose my Lily, both here and in the world to come!"

* * * * *

The Major's story gave the key-note, and ghost story followed ghost story, each more creepy than the last, but a civil engineer was, by common consent, voted "the kettle" for what he called Nadir's Ghost Story. As I decline all responsibility, it is only fair that I should withdraw, and allow my worthy "road scraper" to tell his own tale, and may the Lord have mercy on his soul!

NADIR'S GHOST STORY.

"My wife was in a tantrum, and small blame to her, poor girl. Ninety miles in a dâk ghari with a three-month-old baby in the middle of July, is enough to disturb the equanimity of most people. What with prickly heat, mosquitoes, glare, jibbing ponies, and a howling infant, she had had about enough of it. But the worst was over, and another ten miles in the cool of the evening would have landed us safely in Cawnpore. It was not to be—*l'homme pro-*

pose, la femme dispose—and my wife declined to leave the wretched old dâk bungalow till the next day.

"I wandered away disconsolately into the Compound, and found there my old friend Nadir, the hoary old villain who cooks the withered fowl and goat-like mutton which is served up at all such places as European food.

"'Oh, provider of the poor, your face is as the storm-cloud before the great Bursat (rains). Oho! oho! the Sahib no longer travels on the wings of the wind. He has a clog round his foot now, and takes unequal steps. What, you would give ten rupees to be in Cawnpore to-night?

"'It is good. Let your honour get ready the Paisa, for within an hour will the Mem Sahib gladly flee from this worthless hovel. How will I do it? I am an old man. I have seen many things. Let me tell the Mem Sahib one story—one true story.' And the chuckle which supplied the end of his sentence spoke volumes.

"It was wrong of me, but when I thought of the piles of correspondence awaiting me in Cawnpore I hardened my heart and bade him go to work.

"A few minutes later I could see the old scamp dandling the baby and spouting away at a great rate to the Mem Sahib.

"I sought out a convenient stone, and with the help of my old briar pipe and a copy of the *Pioneer*, awaited coming events patiently.

"Pipe No. 3 was drawing to its sweetest close, when my wife came hurrying out of the house, exclaiming 'Oh, Charlie, dear, do let us get on to Cawnpore. I would not spend the night here for any money.'

"As a dutiful husband, of course, I obeyed her, and we were soon galloping merrily into the cantonments.

"The story with which my wife was frightened out of the dâk bungalow is so strange, and was in such an unexpected way corroborated, that I have resolved to set it down in black and white.

"Whether I personally believed in the power of anything out of spirit-land does not matter. The facts I give are true, draw what inference you may."

"Thirty-two years ago! Wah, wah! I was a man then, the sap was in the tree; now am I dry and fit for fuel. Two-and-thirty years ago, towards sunset, there came a tall English Mem Sahib, dressed all in black, walking swiftly down the Cawnpore road, but Cawnpore lies ten miles away, and English ladies travel not alone on foot! Did I say she was alone? I lied, for in her arms she carried a lovely golden-haired girl, some four years old.

"Strange, I deemed it, to see the lady in such guise, but it was no duty of mine to ask questions, and oven had it been I fear me I dared not have done so, for the strange lady's eyes shone as a cobra's before it strikes.

"She entered the house, and soon retired to rest, a long, long rest, for when we entered the room next morning she lay dead and cold, the babe beside her dead.

"The doctor Sahib said she had first strangled the little one and then poisoned herself.

"Many Sahibs have slept safely in that same room since then, but ill fares it with any child who lies down to rest there! The Mem Sahiba smiles. Native nonsense, eh? Be it so, but will your honour hear what befell Mrs. Tracy and her child two years ago, here in this room, and when you reach Cawnpore ask her have I spoken true words.

"Just two years ago cholera was raging in Cawnpore, and Mrs. Tracy brought her sick child out here for change; the air is purer and the water is sweeter than in cantonments. The child was very ill; fever burnt her little limbs, and she raved and moaned incessantly.

"The mother never flinched or wearied. Day and night she remained by the cot to damp the heated brow and cool the parched lips, and after three days the fever ceased and the child slept soundly. The mother bade me watch awhile so that the ayah and she might snatch some rest, she in a chair, the ayah on the ground.

"All was very still save the distant bark of some pariah dog and the chawkedar's call. The gong at the neighbouring thannah struck twelve, and as ordered I awoke the lady, who instantly bent over the cot to satisfy herself that the child slept soundly. As she again raised herself a look of surprise came over her face, rapidly changing to horror, and oh, merciful Allah! In the doorway, her eyes blazing, her hands outstretched, was the same lady who died here so many years ago.

"She moved rapidly towards the cot, and it was easy to judge from the trembling movement of her fingers that she meant to fasten on the throat of the little one.

"I was paralyzed with terror, and could do nothing to help; the ayah awoke, saw the threatening figure, and grovelled on the ground, covering her head with her sari.

"But Mrs. Tracy, drawing herself up to her full height, stretched her left hand over the cot as if to protect it, and pointing firmly with her right at the advancing figure bade it withdraw.

"For what seemed to me a long time neither moved, but finally the threatening figure drew back little by little and vanished slowly.

"Mrs. Tracy lay back well-nigh exhausted and sadly horror-stricken; but her trials were not yet over, for shortly the child began to moan in her sleep and awoke screaming violently —

"'Oh, mammy, mammy, save me from the black lady!'

"And the poor mother was fain to raise her in her arms to soothe and comfort her.

"Three hours passed, and utterly exhausted by what she had been through, Mrs. Tracy lay fast asleep with the child in her arms. I too had been dozing, but awoke to feel a chill blast passing over me, and again I saw the dark figure, which had now advanced into the room, and was close to the sleeping child; again her eyes burnt with an unholy flame, and again her quivering hands sought the bare neck of the little one.

"I screamed loudly, and Mrs. Tracy awoke. Once more she covered the child with her protecting arm, and waved back the evil visitor.

"I now sprang up, seized a chair and struck with might and main at the figure before me; the chair passed through and through, and was shattered to pieces on the ground, but the evil lady still stood there and glared with hate and disappointed fury.

"As on the previous occasion, she drew back before Mrs. Tracy's steadfast glance step by step till lost to sight.

"How we welcomed the blessed sunlight before whose beams all evil things must flee away!

"The child recovered and is well, but go

and ask Mrs. Tracy why she, a young woman, has hair as white as snow, then will you know that the old Kansamah Nadir has told you a true story.

*   *   *   *   *

"I did see Mrs. Tracy, and asked her the question Nadir suggested; she reluctantly confirmed the above story in every respect.

"Could the cold, lifeless hand of a murderess, long since dead, really have injured the sleeping child? Do spirits of evil hover round us with power to cause physical harm? If we accept the possibility of guardian angels watching over and protecting us it seems scarcely consistent to repudiate the existence of spirits working for our ill.

"Believe as we may, the subject is one deserving more than a passing thought."

"Passing thought be d—d!" said the most irreverent sub. present; "pass the liquor this way."

And it passed more than once, so much so

that it was one o'clock in the morning before we broke up and wended homewards.

Ghost stories, after a skinful of champagne, are the worst possible training for a long ride in the dark, as our party soon found. We were eight in number—five rode, two walked, I, as usual, carried in a jhampan. When halfway through the dense pine forest the leading file stopped suddenly.

"Holy Virgin! What is that figure, robed in white, sitting calmly on the fallen pine yonder? She moves! She —"

But mortal man could stand no more; my bearers dropped me and fled; the riders turned and spurred for life, whilst the two on foot could have given Atalanta ten yards in a hundred.

My best pace being about a mile an hour, it was no use my running away, so I sat still and sweated from fright. The figure now turned towards me.

"Mrs. X., by all that's wonderful!" I tremblingly called out her name.

No answer; but from the other side a voice came through the darkness —

"Where is she? Oh! where is my darling?"

The husband, for his was the voice, came on to where I was, and explained in a few words that his wife was a somnambulist, and this the result.

He awoke her carefully, and we packed her up warmly in my jhampan, whilst the husband hurried off after my fugitive bearers.

The roasting which awaited the runaways was a caution against turning one's back on a ghost.

We had danced, raced and picnicked, but yet our leading spirits would have it that "we took no delight out of ourselves!" and some genius suggested a Christy Minstrel troupe.

"Oh, certainly! Nothing easier! Has anyone any music?"

After much search a torn copy of "Eileen Mavourneen" was discovered.

But a way out of this little trouble was found; a young lady said —

"I can play any accompaniment, if you whistle me the air."

The genial Resident gave us permission to use his piano—the only one in Kashmir—and each performer "whistled his tune."

After sundry rehearsals, nine of us faced a crowded audience, and for two hours kept them in roars. Our corner-men would have been a success anywhere, and peppered the audience with the most personal chaff, from the Resident Sahib down to the fat Parsee tradesman.

Banjo solos and step dancing wound up the entertainment; but the Irishmen made a night of it, and how they all got home alive has ever since been a wonder to me.

The next venture was a *café chantant.* Whew—our barmaids! Such caps and aprons! Such airs and graces; no one served unless he said "My dear," or some term usually employed by the nobility when addressing real live bar ladies. Alas! one husband didn't see it, and, after some winged words, he introduced his bootmaker to the other man's tailor, and the fat was in the fire.

Thus, with cricket, polo, races, and general diversion, we got through July, and were again free to go down into the valley.

Farewell! a long farewell to my log hut! How thoroughly I have enjoyed these two months spent in your snug and cosy walls!

The autumn months in Kashmir are as near perfection as it is possible here below—warm in the daytime, the nights clear and cold.

"Fruit sells for nothing there, if you like to buy," as the old Harrow song puts it—peaches, grapes, apples, pears, custard apples, etc., *ad lib.*

A "dali" of vegetables out of the Resident's garden is a sight to see, but still better are its contents when cooked and served up at that most hospitable table (I refer to the consulship of Mr. Parry Nisbet, to whom Kashmir owes so much!).

Before his time the Maharajah got out of hand, but after some lunging and handling he goes up to his bit very nicely.

Another Englishman who has done good work in Kashmir, though in a different way, is the missionary doctor Neve, of whom it is doubtful whether his skill or his disinterestedness is the greater. Some of his successful operations would cause wonder and dismay among his more conventional brethren, whilst his daily life is worthy of all admiration.

The summer is past and gone, and I still linger lazily in the valley, but as a winter here would not suit me at all I prepare for the march out, when "oh, joy; oh, rapture unforeseen!" the best and kindest of friends, also Murree bound, with a large party, invites me to join on. Instead of long, lonely marches I am in the midst of a joyous band. Golden-haired visions, mounted on dainty little ponies, flit backwards and forwards, laughing, shouting, and enjoying everything. Who are these? You have met them before on a sad occasion, Tweezer's funeral to wit! If lovable in their grief, they are still more so in their happy unconcern and keen enjoyment of the passing hour.

Our party required 80 coolies and 30 mules daily for transport, and at each stage the "tessildar" solemnly assured us he could not supply such a contingent, but persuasion of different kinds did the impossible, and we moved on in triumph.

When the day's march was over kind hands would pile up rugs and cushions to make a soft couch for the invalid, and, when comfortably fixed, three cherubs would perch around him and with one voice exclaim, "Now tell us a story." Bless your baby hearts and angel faces, I should ask nothing better than to lie here for ever, and tell you tales of wonder, watching your big eyes grow bigger, and your rosy cheeks still rosier from excitement.

One of my cherubs had a doll that accompanied her in all her wanderings; a doll I call it, as I want to be polite, and because my cherub allows no levity on this subject. In its original state, ages ago, it had been a little horse, with tail and mane complete, but when first presented to my admiring eyes, it had no legs, no tail, and, *horribile dictu!* no head, but despite of these little drawbacks, the cherub loved this toy madly, fondly, and showered kisses on it in a way to make any poor man envious.

Our daily journey carried us on past Uri, Hattian, Gurri, Dunail, etc., the usual resting places, till after a long 27 miles from Kohalla we sighted Murree, and were soon enjoying the good things of life in Powell's Hotel. Here we taste beef again. In Kashmir, where the rulers are the most bigoted Hindus, killing a cow is a penal offence, and beef there is none. The people are Mahomedans, and, of course, would gladly kill and eat, but the miserable handful of Hindus, thanks to our support, are able to play the tyrant in every way. Personally I should like to see a rebellion in Kashmir and every Hindu flying for his life, after which England could, with a clean conscience, occupy and colonize this delightful country.

Then let the rupee fall to tuppence, what need the retired Anglo-Indian care? His home is in the happy valley, his boys and girls are growing up strong and hardy; no home remittances, no tailor's bills to vex his old heart.

He breeds ponies for the polo market and mules for the Government transport. His wife makes jams, which are sent away into India, where they produce three hundred per cent.

But, alas, none of these dreams can be realized, because we sold Kashmir for fourpence and a postage stamp years ago, and honour forbids us to go back of our bargain. Bah! A nation that disestablished and disendowed the Irish Church need not be so very squeamish about its engagements. Let us give the Maharajah of Kashmir eighteenpence and an unlimited freedom for making a beast of himself, and take back into our own strong hands this possible Eden, this present Hell.

Mercy on us! To what has my slice of beef led me? Kashmir politics; no less. Is the beef responsible, or that second pint of Murree ale? Anyhow, I apologize.

CELIBACY *v.* MATRIMONY.

I am going to put my foot in it; I feel it, I deplore it—a man generally does when he gets talking about abstruse things like marriage without making personal experiment of the subject first. Speaking, then, with abject humility, I say that if a man is bound to spend much of his life in the plains he is far better unmarried. How men can endure seeing their womenfolk droop and fade in that merciless heat is beyond my comprehension.

Man has his work, which keeps him from thinking about heat, or flies, or punkahs, and man has long days in the jungle where the joy of shikar drives away all fret and worry; But what has woman to fill up her life in that darkened house she enters at 8 a.m., not to leave it again till the shadows are long and the sun is low?

All honour and respect to ye fair English matrons who stand by your husbands under hard and trying circumstances, But (again with a capital) how many of ye do so?

A few facts, by your leave.

In winter there are 180 ladies in the station where I lived; in July we sought but only found 18.

In Agra, where some eighty ladies can be reckoned on for a Christmas ball, I have known six only available for some fun we had in September.

But where are the ninety and nine? In the hills?

This brings me to what I am contending for, namely, that as he won't see much of her, a wife is not a desideratum to the ordinary Anglo-Ind. Half a loaf is better than no bread, would be rather a dangerous argument for anyone holding opposite views; to advance, as to complete such a metaphor, he would have to treat his wife like his last crust, which might lead to unpleasantness.

When children make their appearance matters are still worse, for even if the wife should desire to stay in the plains with her husband the mother cannot risk the life of her little one, and the first hot wind of April sees her in full flight to the nearest hill station.

Do you think several months of complete liberty is a good thing for the young married girl who only a couple of years ago was playing with her dolls? Is she quite in a position to decide whether Mrs. Featherhead, with her pleasant ways, is or is not a suitable friend? or whether the attentions of Captain Scapegrace are strictly platonic or not?

It is a common thing to hear people saying, "There is no harm in Mrs. Featherhead; she flirts, but what of that?" Well, of that, nothing; but of her allowing a friend with whom she had flirted to pay Manikchand Rs. 6,000 for her, a good deal.

This paying of bills is far too common, and in a country where nothing is hid leads to deplorable results. I had to examine the books of a rich merchant who has a shop at Mussoorie, and some of the entries were unsavoury.

Of course Mussoorie is the greatest sinner, because there being no Government House there to lead in the paths of order and decorum, the result is that, in the words of a well-known shop-keeper, "there is only one set in Mussoorie, and we are all in it."

I would as soon allow a wife of mine to become a ballet-girl or a Hallelujah lassie as to spend six months at this hill station alone.

Heaven be praised for my jealousy!

But the saddest part of married life only presents itself after some years have elapsed, and the poor wife has to decide whether she will leave her children to be brought up by strangers, or allow her husband to pull through alone, deprived of all those home comforts to which her good house-keeping has accustomed him. Many a poor fellow have I known in this condition, and the term, "fish out of water," best describes them.

No, look at the question as you will, I maintain that matrimony in the plains of India is not a state to be envied.

CHUMMING.

Having decided against matrimony, the six-roomed bungalow feels lonesome and empty, the remedy for which is a chum.

A pleasant, cheery companion who is always ready to ride out of a morning, who has plenty of work all day, and who turns up to his dinner dressed like a gentleman, is the chum for me.

The chum to avoid is a society-darling or professional lady-killer; the brute is never there when wanted, and very much there when *de trop*. I have been very lucky with all my chums, but pre-eminently best was one of whom Rudyard Kipling has told a story in his perfect style. I refer to "Reggy Burke" and the "Bank Fraud."

A hot weather in the plains enables one to take a chum's measure somewhat accurately; if he can keep on bright and jolly when the earth around is a furnace, and cholera is striking down its victims to left and right of him, there is not much wrong with his heart or head.

Some men chum entirely on the live-and-let-live principle, when each goes his own way, has his own friends, and never observes any ceremony with his pal—*chaque un à son gôut*—but I cannot think such a state of things pleasant. Fancy never knowing if you were to dine alone, or be unexpectedly bombarded by friends of your friend?

To prevent any friction between the numerous servants necessarily employed by two bachelors it is best to have the "Sirdar" or head servant in common, and the more he is respected and "bahadured" the better will the joint household succeed.

INAIT KHAN (BEARER).

In my house there was only one lord and master—my bearer, Inait Khan! Not a very imposing person—being somewhat monkey-faced and skinny—but, nevertheless, he ruled us well and wisely. Perhaps the secret of his power lay in the fact that he held the purse, and if either master or servants offended his lordship, supply failed!

He was as unlike the ordinary lying, cowardly servant so common nowadays as chalk to cheese, for though always respectful, he was quite fearless, and would remonstrate forcibly if he deemed me guilty of extravagance or injustice to any other servant (a thing—be it said *en passant*—one is very prone to in a land where servants are many, and orders have to be transmitted *ad lib.*)

From the stately "Kansamah" down to the grubby little dog-boy, all obeyed Inait without a murmur and addressed him as "Sirdar," but were evidently on the best of terms with him. Did "Sukhoo," the syce, want to send home five rupees, Inait filled in the necessary papers. Did Murli, the mehta, want to write and inquire about his sick father, Inait wrote at his dictation. And, again, was it not Inait who got the Sahib to advance Rs. 50 to Amir, the khit, for his wedding, thereby saving him from the money-lender's sixty-two per cent.? As a rule, Inait managed to settle all disputes in the Compound, but on one occasion he failed, and the matter was brought to me. Raheem, khitmugar, accused Gulab, bhisti, of having cast sheep's-eyes at his wife! He fairly howled for vengeance. Gulab repudiated the accusation with scorn, and rudely added that if he was seeking for pearls he would not go search for them on Rahim's manure heap! Whew! They were both strong, able-bodied men, so I ordered a large circle to be formed, and two sticks to be brought—one was handed to Rahim, the other to Gulab. Now, Rahim was a man of war, having, according to his own account, been two years a prisoner in Afghanistan, and the hero of endless blood-thrilling adventures, consequently bhisti was generally considered a gone coon.

The battle only lasted two minutes, and Rahim caved in hopelessly!

There was a grand reconciliation; each side stood treat to the Compound of "metai" (sweets), and peace resumed her sway.

Inait used to have grand rows with the old scamp who supplied the corn for the horses, and the old gentleman came weeping to me on several occasions. A glance at the bazaar rates, of which a copy was sent to me monthly, proved he was "trying it on," so I fined him a rupee, and Inait rejoiced greatly.

When leaving India I asked the little man how much money he had in hand?

"Rs. 120, Sahib."

"What!" said I, "is that all you have saved, you extravagant young rascal, in ten years!"

Whereupon he explained to me that his father, a camel sowar in the Collector's service, had had the misfortune to lose his camel, and been obliged to pay Rs. 350 towards the fund for replacing it. As a dutiful son he had helped.

Any money I gave him would have gone the same way, so, instead of cash, I gave him my photographic kit, the use of which he understands thoroughly, and no one in search of a good bearer need go seek for Inait Khan, as his days of service are ended.

MAGIC.

> "Your vessels and your spells provide
> Your charms and everything beside."
>
> *Macbeth.*

Courts of Law and an active police organization are, doubtless, very useful—nay, indispensable—to the ends of justice, but to the victim of what I may term the common garden thief, immediate detection of the criminal, without having recourse to bobby, bench, or bar, is often of the greatest blessing.

Such an one I would strongly advise to send his bearer for the nearest sorcerer, magician—wise man—give him what name you please, and set him to work to discover the thief.

I was very much amused watching the proceedings of one of these magicians. He first secured the use of an empty mud hut in the Compound, and after obtaining some fire and an empty ghurrah (an earthen vessel used for carrying water) he shut himself up and proceeded to his incantations.

At the end of half-an-hour he emerged and requested all the servants to be seated in a semi-circle round the door, then, beginning with the nearest, he bade him enter the darkened hut and strike three times with open hands on the ghurrah, which was just visible.

Seven men passed the ordeal safely, but the eighth was seized on and denounced as the thief.

The miserable man dropped on his knees, and, confessing his crime, pointed out where he had hidden the money.

The trick was a simple one: whilst busy with his incantations, the sorcerer had found time to carefully blacken the ghurrah. Those whose consciences were sound did as he bade them, and returned with hands well-blackened; the culprit, not knowing what horror the three blows might lead to, had carefully refrained from touching the object indicated, and had consequently reappeared with clean hands.

> "I never had to do with wicked spirits:
> But you . . . .
> Because you want the grace that others have,
> You judge it straight a thing impossible
> To compass wonders, but by help of devils."
>
> *Henry VI.*, Part 1, Act V., Scene 4.

Another method of detecting the criminal is still more simple.

Having made all the servants squat around him in a circle, the sorcerer placed in each of their hands a small quantity of crushed grain, which, at a given signal, they were required to put into their mouths and swallow.

A more amusing spectacle than the thirty men all chewing for bare life can scarcely be imagined. One by one the jaws ceased to work, as man after man completed the allotted task.

But alas for one unfortunate Bhisti! With eyes well-nigh starting out of his head, and fists tightly clenched, he chewed and chewed, but apparently "got no furruder," and began to emit sounds like a half-throttled pig.

Here was the thief, and he himself (after being allowed to remove the dry cake from his mouth) admitted his guilt, and showed where he had concealed the missing article!

Now how had this detection been brought about? Simply by applying a bit of knowledge which any medical man can vouch for the correctness of, namely, that the nervous condition of a man has a very marked effect upon the salivary glands.

The guilty one, especially if he be a native of India, will be in a highly nervous state, and the effect of his fears will be to seal up his salivary glands, and to well-nigh choke him in his attempts to reduce the grain to pulp.

Of course the sorcerer must not repeat the same tricks too often in a neighbourhood, and must show no little cleverness in devising new methods for surprising guilty consciences.

THE CLUB.

Although we cannot in India make much display of an "upper ten thousand," or of "a bloated aristocracy," yet we do our little best to keep up class distinctions, and we do or do not belong to the Club! If we do St. Peter will, without further certificate, admit us into Paradise; if not Hades yawns a greeting.

And yet the ordinary Mofussal Club is not a very formidable affair, being much in the nature of a respectable pothouse, where village wights meet to exchange—"Heaven save the mark"—their ideas.

But be the building ever so humble, it confers none the less the hall mark of respectability, and will probably lead to your forming a "how d'ye do" acquaintance with such swells as the Collector, possibly even with the Commissioner, but this is too much to expect.

Next to having a pretty wife who can and will flirt with the powers that be, the best way to succeed in India is to get the reputation of being a good Club Secretary; it means good stations, and the hills on full pay. I knew a man once who combined a flirting wife to unrivalled powers of managing a Club; he soared to such giddy heights that I should be accused of romancing if the tale of his glory were to be here unfolded.

A room for ladies is always provided, and, strange to say, the further off that room is from the main building the quieter and pleasanter is the Club.

Agra can boast the best Club in the N.W.P., thanks to that ami in time of royalty, the great and good Sir J. No mistake possible; there is but one Sir J., Knt. Had he not been called to greatness in other ways he would have gone down to posterity as the best cook in Asia. Even now, when entertaining crowned heads and lordly T.G.'s, Sir J. never disdains to take off his coat between two courses, and go out to the kitchen, where he gives certain finishing touches; on his return he puts on his coat, wipes his hands on the part of the table-cloth nearest him, and resumes the conversation unconcernedly.

The Allahabad Club is the home of the "sing song." What is a sing song? Oh, ignorance, hearken! It is a clear moonlight night in May; on the lawn in front of the Club some forty or fifty men are seated in long deep chairs, smoking; they have dined, they are happy! The Secretary's voice is now heard, "Gentlemen, have you ordered your favourite poison? If so, I call on Mr. M. to sing 'Father O'Flyn.'" A lazy murmur of approval goes round, and the next minute a rich bass voice booms out the song named; when ended, M. calls on whom he pleases, and so on *ad lib.* All is done comfortably seated, with smoke and drink mighty adjacent.

A BOBBERI PACK.

Some of the jolliest mornings I have ever spent have been when scampering after a good big jackal, which is the most usual victim pursued by that strange collection of mongrels dignified by the title of bobberi pack; but foxes are often run into, and on rare occasions an old grey wolf has kindly offered his services.

The pack of which I was joint owner with a chum consisted of two half-bred Rampore hounds, huge lean savages; two unadulterated village pariah dogs, never sick or sorry; three animals which, when presented to us, were termed retrievers, and which out of politeness we continued to call so; and, finally, an ever-varying number of leggy fox terriers. Musical, m' yes, a little too musical; but yoicks! gone away! Don't stand there doing the captious critic, but let your horse rip, and look ahead for concealed nullahs and other pitfalls.

We started from home at 4.45 a.m., thus can hunt for nearly two hours; then home to chota haziri and tubs, and so to work by eight o'clock, feeling very fit and beany.

The keep of this noble pack of hounds, together with their feeder's pay, cost us about Rs. 80 a month. If any M.F.H. would like a few tips on economy we shall be delighted to favour him!

VOLUNTEERS.

"This ain't all beer and skittles, swelp me Bob," said our smart-looking Sergeant-Instructor, as he wiped the sweat from his brow, and the panting flanks of our horses fully attested the truth of his remark.

We rather fancied ourselves across country, in the Volunteer Light Horse; our only General called it scouting, but we were not proud, and contented ourselves with riding friendly steeplechases on all possible and impossible occasions, which no doubt brought in much valuable information.

But despite such occasional frivolity, we used to do good hard drill, and if ever called on, the Volunteers of India, whether cavalry or infantry, will be found ready and steady.

Some very justifiable pressure is brought to bear on men to make them join; every Englishman in India ought to be a Volunteer, and efficient.

For instance, it is wonderful how soon the services of railway servants are dispensed with if they fail to join the corps and learn their drill smartly; as a result, there are now several lines that could turn out seven to eight hundred strong. The telegraph department is also very loyal, and, considering the long hours of work they have to put in, it is wonderful how much drill they attend. But for gentle pressure nothing can touch the opium department. Now the opium department is one and indivisible. It is called "Lord Harry," and Lord Harry is a volunteer down to the tips of his fingers, who, when his noble charger stands still, looks imposing; if, however, the luckless animal moves on, Lord H. falls off, and sends an article to the *Pioneer* describing the accident. But what of that? Centaurs are quite out of fashion.

Memories of '57 ought to make every Englishman in India willing and anxious to learn how to defend himself and those dear to him in time of danger.

The blatant Bengali Babu papers are very fond of advocating the employment of natives as volunteers; the idea tickled the Mahomedan population immensely, and was finely treated by that splendid old man Syed Ahmed of Allyghur in a speech which every globe-trotting M.P. would do well to read before swallowing neat all the bosh his Congress friends offer him to slake his thirst for knowledge.

If these good gentlemen could converse with such men as the Syed their subsequent remarks in Parliament would be of more value, but that, alas, is impossible, as the

Syed does not speak English, and is not the sort of man to stand conversation through an interpreter. It will be a noble sight when Calcutta can produce a native volunteer corps, but arrangements must be made to prevent the noise of firearms or I sadly fear the gallant Babu warriors will right-about-face in double quick time. If a troop of light horse could be added the riding of Mr. Winkle will soon be surpassed.

THE GYMKANA.

The Gymkana is a living thing; it is the true and only source of all rational exercise and amusement; what it means I don't know, but if you do not belong to it you are a "bounder" and an "outsider," two most objectionable persons.

Pay the rather stiff entrance fee, and look as though you liked it; as your reward you are sure of having lawn tennis, cricket, racquets, badminton, rowing, and polo to your heart's content.

This seems a fair amount for your money, but you may add to it a little local race meeting fortnightly, and probably an open meeting three or four times a year.

How it is all done for the money puzzles many a one, but a good Gymkana manager will have a year's sport, and present a nice little balance in hand, which must promptly be spent in giving a rattling dance.

It doesn't take long to die in India, and, as a natural consequence, men "take all the delight out of themselves possible," to which wisdom the local gym. is the best help.

PICNICS.

A picnic is either the dullest form of amusement or the jolliest, but I am free to confess it is generally the former. I remember how a young lady managed to enliven a return journey from a deadly performance; we were all riding, and she was splendidly mounted. She whispered to me,

"I am going to be run away with; tell some of the others." I did so, and a few minutes later, when she screamed and headed for the open country, we yelled like red Indians and chivied hard; but in vain, and she gave us twenty minutes of good going. Her wonderful escape was the local topic of conversation for many days; also we, her pursuers, were much blamed for following so close behind a runaway. We apologized. Oh, that gunners' picnic, where after gorging and guzzling horribly, we all played hunt the slipper. "*Mon ami*, have you evair play hunt ze slippair, *c'est magnifique!*" But as a set off, there was that awful river picnic when the tug broke down, and instead of being home at six p.m. we crawled in at 11.30; the liquor failed about eight o'clock, all but a bottle of curaçoa, which was greedily finished by a gallant plunger, whose conversation then became such that we had to place a pillow on his head and take it in turns to sit on it.

SWEETHEARTS.

Alas! that the plural should be necessary. But they do grow so fast, and then a stern mamma takes them away to a horrid place called England, and never again will the lonely bachelor be allowed to kiss and worship them. But others follow fast, and fickle mankind is consoled.

My most serious affair was with a golden-headed maiden, who, for reasons unknown, christened me "my darlin'." Pardon the "g;" she was just three years old, and a "g" or an "r" were things she despised. No shy or bashful maiden this; openly she appropriated me and mine.

"I'se comin' to tea with you, my darlin'; what cake shall you have?" or else it was, "You send Ayah home and take me for a dwive!" But when before a room full of people she gravely said, "I must go now or else my darlin' will not be able to see me in my bath," a rapid retreat became necessary to save my blushes.

Kathleen Mavourneen, better known as "Her Serene Highness," next played the deuce with my feelings. Though little over two years old, she was a finished coquette, and somewhat inclined to tyranny. The way she bullied her dad was a caution, and her brethren bowed in slavish submission to her behests. The little monkey was almost too beautiful, and unless she takes to green spectacles, her great violet eyes will do terrible execution sixteen years from now.

When pleased with my general conduct, H.S.H. allowed me to sit beside her at dinner and gaze respectfully at her dainty feeding, but at other times I was sternly told to "Do 'way, 'orrid man!"

After the daily game of lawn tennis, Kathleen often honoured me by "dwivin' my geegees home," and very important the mite looked holding the end of the reins. But one luckless day I ventured to give a lady friend a lift, and called out for H.S.H. She toddled up, ayah and bearer escorted as usual, caught sight of the fair intruder, then with withering scorn she hurled these words at me, "U'se got another lady; I shan't tome!" My infidelity was not forgiven till the present of a small gazello restored me to favour some weeks later.

In startling contrast to this imperious little lady was the romping Daisy; no courtly airs and graces here, but, instead, a warm and sympathetic heart. How gentle the four-year-old maiden could be no one but the invalid mother knew; how deftly the little hands placed the damp handkerchiefs on the burning brows and fanned and petted her "sweetest mummie" was hidden from other eyes. The Daisy we knew was the fearless little rider who bucketed her father's polo ponies across country, and entertained a sovereign contempt for anyone who funked.

Having heard us one day discussing whether or not to blister the foreleg of a black pony, rightly christened "Shaitan," a kicking, biting, fiendish animal, she made tracks for his stall, and, to our horror, knelt down and gravely examined the groggy limb. To rush forward and drag her away would have been fatal; Shaitan stood like a lamb, and after awhile Daisy got up and came back to us. We went into the house and took it neat.

May a rich and honourable man some day have the good luck to marry Daisy.

Alas! what can I tell about my last sweetheart. Her face that of an angel, but *horribile dictu,* there issued from those dainty little lips floods of vile, low Hindustani, such as is used by low-class sweepers. Her mother was a beauty, and, not to be in the way of admirers, the poor child was constantly left with the servants, and naturally picked up their ways and words. She did not, thank God, understand fully the hideous nature of what she said. It was terribly sad.

Did I say that mothers carried away all our sweethearts beyond the seas? Would that it were so; but, alas! the thousand little graves, with their piteous words of tender farewell, are silent witnesses to the contrary. A careless moment, during which Sunnylocks escapes joyfully from the darkened nursery, to revel a brief while in the bright sunshine yonder, pursuit, and capture; surely no harm can ensue. Towards evening the little maid grows listless, and father hears no joyous welcome as he returns from the long day's work. Fever, burning, consuming, destroying fever seizes the little victim, and ere morning the weeping mother hears the gentle, fluttering sigh which tells her all is over. Hush! dear one, hush! and ere it be too late, turn those tear-stained eyes heavenward. See the silver gleaming of that angel's wings. See how tenderly our little one is held in those bright arms, and how she smiles—free now and for ever from pain or care.

These bitter moments burn so deeply in a mother's heart that years after a word, a song, may recall the scene, and, amid brightness and laughter, bring unbidden tears to her eyes.

HOMEWARD BOUND.

Hurrah! and again, hurrah! Once more a bright, clean P. and O. liner welcomes us; once more the fresh salt air washes the indescribable smell of India out of our nostrils; once more may we drink bottled bass without fear of to-morrow's avenging liver. We are all as sober as judges till Aden, when young Australia comes on board, and then we sober old Anglo-Indians get infected with the super-abundant life and spirits then imported, and rollick and frolic with the best.

Bless those jolly, broad-shouldered, red-cheeked Colonials; what good fellows they are! They challenged India, as they termed our contingent, to a cricket match, and beat us horribly; then to a shooting competition, wherein they were beaten and lost much of their superfluous cash; then to a tug-of-war, to football, to ship's quoits, to chess, and to heaven only knows what else.

Having crawled up the Canal by electric light, we touched at Port Said for a few hours. Just the time to go into the Eldorado and tempt Miss Fortune at the roulette table. Losers said little, but the few winners rejoiced greatly in the spoil. Our purser twice scooped in the oof on a single number, and, like a wise man, departed with his gains.

At Brindisi, amidst much popping of champagne corks and "hope to see you again, old fellow," the majority of the Indian contingent leave the good ship, and speed on across the continent—homeward bound!

FINIS.